Best-kept Secrets of the Women's Institute

JAMS, PICKLES & CHUTNEYS

Midge Thomas

First published in Great Britain by Simon & Schuster UK Ltd, 2002
A Viacom Company

Simon & Schuster UK Ltd
Africa House
64–78 Kingsway
London
WC2B 6AH

1 3 5 7 9 10 8 6 4 2

Design and typesetting: **Fiona Andreanelli**
Food photography: **Steve Baxter**
Home economist: **Sara Buenfeld**
Stylist for food photography: **Liz Belton**
Editor: **Deborah Savage**
Printed and bound in China

ISBN 0 74322 113 3

ACKNOWLEDGEMENTS

I am indebted to my Dad (95 this year – 2002) for his love, support and encouragement in everything I have set out to do.

To my husband, Roy, for his patience during the writing of this book and all the other projects which have challenged me throughout our marriage.

To all family and friends for their support. To all the contributors to the book who responded so willingly to my request for recipes.

To Dilwen Phillips for her gentle persuasion, help and reassurance. To Terry Clarke for her friendship and inspiration.

CONTENTS

5   FOREWORD

6   INTRODUCTION

23   SPRING PRESERVES

29   SUMMER PRESERVES

41   AUTUMN PRESERVES

61   WINTER PRESERVES

71   ALL-YEAR-ROUND PRESERVES

78   INDEX OF RECIPES

80   USEFUL ADDRESSES

FOREWORD

Welcome to this book; I hope you will enjoy reading it and be encouraged to try the recipes. There is something very cheering and pleasurable about gazing along a shelf of preserves that you have created. The colours and textures, as well as the tastes, are reminders of the raw ingredients, how you came about them and the seasons of the year. This is why I have arranged the recipes into chapters representing the four seasons – also I suppose to reassure myself that they do still exist despite the vagaries of our weather!

My memories go back to watching and helping my Mum make preserves and I well remember her 'turn' with the WI canning machine back in the early fifties! Little did I know that I would end up passing on information about preserves to WI members at Denman College. I have always dabbled in making preserves, through college days, early married and family times, WI Markets and on into teaching. I enjoy trying new recipes but relish the opportunity of repeating those which have been handed down over generations or bringing a basic recipe bang up to date with a new twist.

Preserving is a very satisfying pastime, which enables us to make a vast array of goodies full of flavour, made from natural ingredients and with no artificial preservatives and gelling agents. We can rely on the favourite traditional varieties or extend our scope using the many different fruits and vegetables that are now available. Some of the recipes in this book may use ingredients you are not familiar with but it is worth seeking them out and trying them. Finding them out is a pleasure in itself – visit your local markets, WI Markets and Farmers' Markets. If you're on the Internet it may be worth a browse there to find small businesses who deliver to your door.

Preserving may be a bit of a mystery to some folk. Someone asked me only the other day what the difference is between a jam and a marmalade. One of the recipes sent to me was called a chutney when it is really a pickle! So the next section (page 6) takes a brief look at the different categories, to help us determine the various ingredients and methods used.

Preserving need not be out of bounds because you don't have the right equipment. A checklist of the equipment you need (page 14) shows that most of it is already to be found in most kitchens. The more expensive items, such as food processors and microwaves, can be a boon and save time and energy and are well worth saving for, as they will be useful in other types of cookery. Other types of preserves may demand more specialist equipment.

And, finally, Techniques for Making Successful Preserves (page 16) gives a host of hints, tips and shortcuts that I have collected over the past few years and gleaned from friends with leanings towards preserve-making. I would like to thank all of them for responding to my request for help in collecting this wonderful range of recipes for you to try. Many of the recipes have passed down through generations and it feels good to be part of the process of keeping these traditions well preserved.

This poem is dedicated to them. It was found in an ageing cookbook by members of Stoneclough WI in Lancashire, who included it in their WI's book of recipes.

RECIPE FOR PRESERVING FRIENDS

Select those with round hearts.
Don't bruise with unfeeling words.
Add a heartful of the milk of human kindness
and plenty of tact.
Warm with sympathy.
Don't overheat or it may ferment mischief.
Knead with oil of unselfishness
but beware of jars.
Keep in a warm corner of the heart.

Years will improve the flavour of this preserve.

INTRODUCTION

A Few Things to Consider Before You Begin

It really does pay to think and plan ahead; make sure you have everything you need, from ingredients to jars and coverings and any equipment – in sufficient quantities. Get everything out ready and organise it so everything you need is to hand when you need it.

Allow plenty of time to complete the recipe and don't attempt too much at any one time. Juggling two or three recipes can get a bit fraught!

Remember to safeguard your health and safety at all times, by observing basic hygiene and simple safety guidelines. This is important during all stages of making preserves and particularly if the process is a lengthy one – such as jelly-making, where the pulp is left to drip for several hours. For basic hygiene information, contact your local authority's Environmental Health Officer or, for guidelines and more details about all aspects of food preservation, read the HMSO publication *Home Preservation of Fruit and Vegetables* (see page 80 for address).

It's very easy to burn yourself when making preserves if you aren't careful. The final mixtures will be extremely hot and dangerous to handle, so take sensible precautions when lifting pans of hot liquid and when transferring from pan to jar. Always use oven gloves (not a tea-towel!) to handle hot pans and plan a sensible system of work: allow space for setting down the hot pan as close to the hob as possible and then arrange a 'production line' for filling the jars so you have to move around as little as possible. Keep children and animals out of the kitchen while you are working as they could be a danger to you and themselves.

Do take extra care when boiling mixtures, especially those with a high proportion of sugar. One of the essential processes in obtaining a set in jams, jellies and marmalades is bringing the mixture to a 'rolling boil', which can result in some of the mixture splashing out of the pan. To avoid this, use a pan large enough to allow the jam to boil vigorously without splashing. The pan should only be about half full when the sugar has been added. It is sensible to wear long sleeves and to protect your hand with an oven mitt when stirring the preserve. It is also a good idea to make sure you aren't wearing open-toed shoes!

In the event of a burn, place the affected area immediately under a running cold tap and keep it there for at least 10 minutes or as long as practical. Then dry carefully and cover with a dry dressing, if necessary.

Obtain immediate medical help if the burn is severe or covers a large area.

Another point worth mentioning is that the manufacturers of ceramic hobs do warn about the effect of spilling hot, high-sugar food on the hob: wipe any splashes up immediately; do not leave them on the surface.

Traditional Raspberry Jam (page 32)

METHODS OF PRESERVING

'**Preserves**' is a general term used to describe fruits and vegetables that have been preserved with the use of heat and sugar and/or vinegar and then stored in sealed jars. The preserves we are concentrating on in this book can be divided into two categories: sugar preserves and vinegar preserves.

SUGAR PRESERVES

Jam is fruit and sugar cooked to form a gel. ACID + PECTIN + SUGAR = GOOD SET. Jams should be clear and bright, characteristic in colour and well set but not too stiff; they should have a distinct fruity flavour.

Conserve is similar to jam except that the set is much softer and some fruits remain whole.

Jelly uses only the fruit juice, after the removal of skin and so on. Because only the juice is used, the yield of a jelly is much lower than that of jam, making it rather more expensive. It is usually made and potted in small amounts and should be clear and sparkling.

Jellies can be served in the same way as jam or they make a wonderful accompaniment to roast or cold meats.

Jellies are often flavoured with herbs – try oregano, sage, sprigs of thyme or rosemary. They are sometimes spiced with cinnamon or cloves and different fruits are often combined to give really interesting-sounding and-tasting results. Try raspberry and blackcurrant together – a delicious variation.

Marmalade is a jam-like preserve, usually made with citrus fruits; a combination of citrus and other fruits is also possible. Marmalade includes peel, which means it takes longer to cook. It uses more water.

Many people would say that the only way to make marmalade is with fresh seville oranges in the very short season which runs from January into February. Purists would expect the peel to be finely cut and the marmalade made to the traditional method. This, of course, is not always possible and there are many different recipes around now to suit all palates and tastes. In this book you will find a traditional recipe with variations (page 63), a quick version which is chopped in the food processor and cooked in the microwave (page 68), another using a pressure cooker (page 70) and other recipes for marmalades using a combination of citrus and other fruits. The basics remain the same.

Butter is usually made when there is a glut of fruit. Fruit butters use less sugar than jam, are softer than fruit cheeses and are usually spiced.

Fruit cheeses are usually served in the same way as dairy cheeses, in wedges. They are cooked to a stiff consistency and set in moulds.

Curd is not a true preserve and not intended for keeping. Curds contain eggs and butter in addition to fruit and sugar and the cooking temperature, compared to other preserves, is very low. For this reason, curds should only be covered with a waxed disc and cellophane cover and they should be refrigerated. Curds can be stored in the refrigerator for up to six weeks. Once opened, they should be eaten within two weeks. (I make lemon curd for my WI Market and the labelling information in the official WI Markets Handbook follows these guidelines.) An alternative method of storing is to pour the curd into small freezer containers and freeze it.

Lemon curd is a particular favourite but other citrus fruits and more exotic fruits can be used. They all make delicious spreads for breakfast and tea-time and can be used for filling cakes and tarts. See under different chapters for each season.

The traditional way to make curd is to cook it in the top of a double-boiler or in a bowl placed over a pan of hot water. Curds can be made very successfully in the microwave, which cuts down the cooking time considerably, and this method is explained in the recipes (see, for example, Lemon Curd, page 24).

WHEN IS A JAM NOT A JAM?

This is a good question, because buying a commercial jam from the supermarket shelf is quite a testing experience – not least, understanding the labels! I hope by the time you've read this book you'll be making your own preserves but here's a quick guide to the EC regulations that govern the sale of jam. If you don't make your own, look for your nearest WI Market or Farmers' Market, where you'll find excellent jams that contain no additives.

Standard jam contains a minimum of 35 g fruit and 60 g sugar per 100 g jam. It can contain colourings, preservatives, citric acid, gelling agent and added pectin.

Extra jam contains a minimum of 45 g fruit + 60 g sugar per 100 g jam. It must be made from whole fruit, not fruit concentrate. No colourings, preservatives or flavourings are allowed. Citric acid, gelling agent and pectin are allowed.

Reduced-sugar jam or **jam with no added sugar** has a minimum of 35 g fruit but only 30–55 g sugar per 100 g jam. Colourings, emulsifiers, stabilisers and preservatives are allowed.

Fruit spreads have no official standard but are usually a fruit pulp sweetened with fruit juice.

Fruit conserve also has no official definition but is often taken to refer to a 'quality' jam with a high fruit content. The fruit is usually steeped in sugar prior to cooking, so that the fruit remains whole. The pectin cannot be released in the usual way during this process; therefore, conserve has a 'soft set' but a superb flavour. Favoured by the French and usually eaten with croissants or scooped up on to chunks of baguette – lovely! – but even better when you've made it yourself.

LOW-SUGAR AND SUGAR-FREE JAMS

Although jams are traditionally made with a high quantity of sugar, some people need to reduce their sugar intake either for health or weight-control reasons and some people simply prefer a fruitier and less sweet flavour. There are a couple of recipes along these lines in All-Year-Round-Preserves (see page 72). A WI friend, Christine Sherriff, gave me these recipes, which she makes regularly.

Remember that such jam will not set so firmly and, more importantly, will not keep for more than a few weeks, because of the reduced level of sugar. Store in a cool, dark place, refrigerate once opened and use within 3–4 weeks of opening. Make these jams in small quantities and put them into small jars, to minimise the 'shelf-life' problem.

DIABETIC JAMS

I have no experience of making jams for diabetics. For further information, contact Diabetes UK (see page 80). In principle, sorbitol and fructose can be substituted for ordinary sugar in preserve recipes. Use the same quantity of sorbitol as sugar but only half the amount of fructose, as it has almost twice the sweetening power. Or try adapting conventional recipes by reducing the sugar by a quarter, that is, use 450 g (1 lb) of fruit to 350 g (12 oz) of sugar. Because they do not contain the same amount of sugar, diabetic jams will not keep as well as ordinary ones; take the same precautions as for other low-sugar jams.

FREEZER JAMS

These eliminate the process of boiling the fruit and sugar together. They rely on the addition of commercial fruit pectin to achieve a 'set'. The finished jam retains all the flavour and texture of the fruit. Strawberries and raspberries are the usual fruits used for freezer jam. Mash or sieve 675 g (1½ lb) of raspberries or strawberries and stir in 900 g (2 lb) of caster sugar. Leave for 20 minutes, stirring occasionally, and then add 100 ml (4 fl oz) of liquid pectin (available from larger supermarkets and chemists) and stir for 3 minutes. Spoon into small rigid plastic containers, cover tightly and label. Leave at room temperature for 24 hours to allow the mixture to gel before freezing. To serve, thaw at room temperature for 1 hour. Keep in the freezer for up to six months.

VINEGAR PRESERVES

Pickles In *clear pickles*, such as pickled onions, salt or brine is used to extract water from the vegetables, leaving them really crisp. They are then packed in vinegar, which can be plain, spiced or sweet.

Sweet pickles, such as damsons, are fruit or vegetables stewed in sweetened, spiced vinegar.

In *mixed pickles*, such as piccalilli, vegetables are brined and then cooked in thickened spiced vinegar.

All pickles need to be covered with vinegar-proof lids.

Chutney A traditional cooked chutney is very straightforward to make; it can be based on almost any combination of fruit and vegetables but it always contains acid, spices and a sweetener. In India, where chutney originated, the word refers to a wide range of products, from a slow-cooked variety that is matured for several weeks to a simple relish made from raw ingredients and eaten within a few hours. In this country, however, chutneys are usually cooked slowly to a jam-like consistency, then matured in the jar for a few weeks before use, to produce a mellow but fruity flavour full of character. They are mainly served with cold meats and cheeses but make a useful accompaniment to other dishes and as an additional flavouring in many other recipes.

A stainless-steel pan is ideal for both chutney and pickles, which contain a high concentration of acid. A thick, heavy base prevents hot spots and protects the preserve from burning.

The vinegar used must be of good quality and one containing not less than 5% acetic acid. Any type of vinegar is suitable; some people prefer to use a wine or cider variety for the fruity flavour, although these are more expensive than malt vinegars.

Both whole and ground spices can be used in chutneys but, for a clear and bright finish, use whole spices tied in a muslin bag – this is then removed before potting.

Covers for chutneys must be vinegar-proof and of the type to prevent evaporation. The most suitable cover is the twist top (see page 14).

Relish contains similar ingredients to chutney but has a different texture and uses less vinegar. The vegetables for a relish are usually more coarsely chopped and are cooked for a shorter time or not cooked at all; therefore the texture has some of the crispness of the original. Because the proportion of vinegar and sugar is low in comparison to chutneys, relishes are not true preserves and they do not keep well for long. They can be eaten immediately after making and, once opened, should be kept in the fridge, for no more than 2–3 weeks.

Sauce has similar ingredients to chutney but is sieved to a purée. Those sauces made with vegetables that are low in acid, such as tomato- and mushroom-based ones, are likely to ferment during storage unless the bottles are processed to sterilise the contents and to form a vacuum seal.

Fruit and herb vinegar contains fruit or herbs simply steeped in vinegar. These vinegars are used for dressings and sauces or may be sweetened for use in drinks and puddings and as a sore throat remedy. (See Raspberry Vinegar, page 38).

Other methods of making preserves are: salting; drying; freezing; curing; smoking; candying; crystallising; canning and bottling – but these are all beyond the scope of this book!

Cranberry Chutney (page 69)

INGREDIENTS FOR PRESERVING

SUGARS

Refined **cane** and **beet sugars** are both suitable for preserves – there is no difference in the keeping quality. Any type of sugar can be used – granulated, caster, cubed or brown – but **granulated sugar** is probably the most widely used and the cheapest. **Preserving sugar** is specially made with large crystals but is more expensive than ordinary sugar. Its main advantage is that it produces less scum and therefore less wastage; it also tends to give a clearer and brighter result – ideal if you enter preserves into competitions at village or WI Federation shows. Special **jam sugar** contains pectin and acid, which helps the preserve to set better than one made with ordinary sugar, but preserves made with this tend to have a more limited shelf life than those made with ordinary sugar. Store for no more than six months and, once opened, keep them in the fridge and eat within 3–4 weeks. Check regularly for any signs of deterioration.

Demerara sugar has a crunchy texture and a distinctive, crystalline appearance; it is available in both refined and unrefined versions. **Muscovado** sugars are raw cane sugars which are softer in texture than demerara and are available in varying shades of brown, usually light or dark. Their pronounced flavour may override those of other ingredients, so this needs to be considered when choosing which kind of sugar to use.

Organic and **unrefined** sugars are now widely available. Unrefined sugars are very simply processed and retain the natural colour and flavour of the molasses in the sugar. Organic sugar is produced without the use of chemicals and will be certified by the Soil Association. These sugars also tend to have a pronounced flavour and this may be detectable in the finished preserve: whether this is desirable or not is a matter for the individual cook to decide. Recipes usually give guidance on which sugar gives the best result.

VINEGARS

Vinegar is the result of an organic process that occurs when a fruit-based or grain-based alcoholic brew is exposed to air; a bacterial reaction turns the alcohol into acetic acid. It is important that vinegar used for pickling should have an acetic acid content of at least 5%; this will be stated on the label. In this high-acid environment, bacteria cannot survive.

Malt vinegar is fermented from malted barley and wine or cider vinegars are fermented from fruit sugars. **Distilled vinegar** is colourless and, therefore, does tend to give a better appearance to many pickles. The brown colour in malt vinegar comes from caramel and does not necessarily indicate that the vinegar is stronger. Wine and cider vinegars are sharper; they have a higher acid content than distilled vinegar. **Pickling malt vinegar** is readily available from shops and supermarkets, pre-flavoured with pickling spices ready for use. Choice of vinegar, like sugar, is a matter of balancing individual preference and what the recipe recommends.

SALT

Salt is a powerful dehydrator, that is, it can extract moisture from fruit and vegetables, leaving them nicely crisp, which is ideal for preserves such as pickles. Salt is either mined from rocks (rock salt) or extracted from sea water (sea salt).

Sea salt has coarse crystals (available in various sizes) and is stronger in flavour than the more common, free-flowing variety and is favoured for preserving methods such as curing and brining. **Cooking salt** is an all-purpose salt. **Table salt** contains anti-caking ingredients and can cause clouding, but this is not a problem in most of the recipes in this book, in which salt is used only for flavouring. Sea salt is purer than table salt.

FRUIT & VEGETABLES

Select the largest and freshest-looking **citrus fruit** for preserves. They should not be bruised or wrinkled and the skin should have a soft shine. If you want them for the peel, look out for unwaxed or organic fruits. You will need to give citrus fruit a good scrub under running water to remove any dirt and fungicide: a tiny drop of washing up liquid will help, followed by a thorough rinse.

Buy the freshest **soft fruit** possible and choose some that is slightly under-ripe. It should be firm and dry. Avoid over-ripe fruit as it will contain relatively more water and less pectin.

Don't waste the citrus peel that you take off fruit for eating or prepare for fruit salads: it makes excellent and economical marmalade. Make sure you scrub the peel first and then pop it in a bag and freeze until you have the right weight of peel for making up the recipe. For Allen's Citrus Fruit Marmalade (page 76), you'll need to save 675 g (1 1/2 lb).

If you are short of time, **commercially prepared fruit**, such as oranges, is a boon. The fruit is prepared, cooked and canned, ready for you to add the sugar and cook to setting point. Many people have said to me over the years I was involved in WI Markets: 'why spend all that time preparing oranges by hand when you can buy them all ready prepared in a tin?' Why indeed! It was while I was National Chairman of WI Markets back in the early 90s that the momentous decision was taken to officially allow WI Market cooks to sell marmalade made from the canned oranges. Some people actually prefer the taste of this marmalade and request it in our WI Markets up and down the country. I have been sent some variation ideas from a Lincolnshire Markets colleague, which you will find on page 77.

Choose fresh young **vegetables** for pickling. Vegetables for chutneys can be damaged or bruised specimens as long as the unsound part is cut away.

You may come across some recipes which use '1 large onion'. Generally speaking, 'large' means a weight of about 225–275 g (8–10 oz).

Both fruit and vegetables can sometimes come in gluts at the height of the season. This is often the best time to buy, both for flavour and cheapness and, if you grow your own, preserving is often the only way to avoid wastage. But you may not have time to embark on a mammoth preserving session just when crops are at their peak. If you haven't time to use produce in season, weigh it out into useable amounts and freeze to use later. This is particularly useful for something like seville oranges for marmalade, which have a short season. Another useful tip when making marmalade is to freeze the reduced oranges and water and then finish when you choose to. Remember to allow extra fruit when you come to use it, as the pectin content of frozen fruit will be less.

You may feel that the recipes given are too large in quantity for your needs – not everyone can cope with 10 jars of every preserve they wish to make! Don't be afraid to halve or quarter the quantities given to get the amount you want.

EQUIPMENT FOR MAKING PRESERVES

Most preserves need little specialist equipment, except perhaps a preserving pan, and can be made satisfactorily with items found in most kitchens. Any equipment you need to buy is widely available from good kitchen shops and stores like Lakeland Ltd, who also supply by mail order and via the Internet. See Useful Addresses, page 80, for suppliers of preserving equipment by mail order or online.

EQUIPMENT CHECKLIST

ESSENTIAL EQUIPMENT:

preserving pan, with sloping sides (see opposite)
• **variety of bowls and basins • plates**
• **colander • nylon sieve • funnel**
• **small and large knives • tablespoons**
• **variety of jars and containers • coverings and labels • thermometer • scales**
• **measuring jug • measuring spoons**
• **wooden spoons • chopping board**

USEFUL BUT NOT ESSENTIAL EQUIPMENT:

juicer or extractor
• **liquidiser/food processor**
• **pressure cooker • microwave cooker**
• **slow cooker • mincer**

INVEST IN A GOOD PRESERVING PAN

A preserving pan is essential for its shape and size. A heavy-based pan of good quality stainless steel will last a lifetime and it is worth paying as much as you can. The heavy base will help to prevent burning – there's nothing more annoying when making preserves than finding a batch of nearly-ready jam is 'catching' on the bottom. The scorched bits soon spread around the batch and impair the flavour. It is also an advantage to have a pan with a lip for easier pouring.

The sloping sides and hence wider top to the pan helps the evaporation process, which is vital for reducing the preserve to the right concentration for a good set and good keeping qualities.

The size is important to allow the mixture to come to a rolling boil without boiling over and being a safety hazard.

The pan should only be about half full when the sugar has been added.

JARS

Most jars are reuseable. If you are short of jars for the amount of preserves you want to make, ask friends, relatives and neighbours to save empty jars for you.

If you still haven't enough, you will have to buy a quantity of jars. I use a company in London that is very good at supplying small amounts and are very helpful on the telephone when ordering. Ring them for a brochure first. As well as plain jars, they also sell hexagonal and octagonal ones that look very attractive to fill and give as gifts at Christmas. The smaller sizes come supplied with the correct-size lids. (See Useful Addresses, page 80.)

COVERS

For general use, a supply of 63 mm twist tops and waxed discs and cellophane covers will be sufficient. DO NOT use both. It is a common mistake to put a waxed disc and a twist top – the waxed disc will prevent the twist top from forming a correct seal.

The cheapest way to cover jams, jellies and marmalades is to use a waxed disc and cellophane cover which is secured with a rubber band. These are available in different sizes from most supermarkets, stationers and kitchen shops, to fit 450 g (1 lb) and 900 g (2 lb) jars.

These are not suitable for chutneys and other vinegar preserves, however, as they are not vinegar-proof since they do not prevent evaporation. The twist-top type of lid is ideal instead, as it is usually lined with plastic, which prevents the vinegar from coming into contact with the metal. They are widely available from kitchenware departments and shops. Scrupulously clean them before use: wash them in hot, soapy water and then rinse well. Then I pour boiling water over them and leave them in it for a few seconds before draining and drying thoroughly.

Top: Cinnamon Grape Pickle (page 51); bottom: Spiced Apple Jelly (page 43)

TECHNIQUES FOR MAKING SUCCESSFUL PRESERVES

STERILISING JARS

This is an essential procedure as you need to eliminate all contamination, such as from the previous contents of the jar, which could cause the new batch of preserve to go off more quickly. Sterilising is especially important if you are using a jar that has contained a vinegar preserve, as you don't want the smell to linger and spoil the next batch of contents. The new preserve will look so much better in a nice clean and shiny jar. It is best to sterilise jars just before you are going to use them.

If you are re-using old jars, check for any chips or cracks and then wash the jars and remove any old labels. Thoroughly wash the jars in hot, soapy water. Just soaking in the hot water may remove labels cleanly or you may need to use something to remove any deposits of adhesive from the previous label. A very good product is called 'Sticky Stuff Remover', which has lots of other uses in addition to getting rid of the stickiness sometimes left after soaking a label off. (It's available from Lakeland, see Useful Addresses, page 80.)

Rinse the jars well in boiling water and turn upside-down to drain. Place on a cooling rack on a pad of kitchen paper and heat in the oven at 160°C/325°F/Gas Mark 3 for 10 minutes or until thoroughly dry. Leave to cool before filling.

Or place the jars in a deep pan and cover with boiling water. Bring to the boil and boil for 10 minutes. Carefully remove and allow to drain and dry as above.

It is possible to sterilise jars in the microwave; follow the manufacturer's instructions for your model. The general method is: half fill the jars with water and heat on full power until the water boils. Use oven gloves to remove the jars from the oven, swirl the water round inside them, and then throw away the water (or into your washing-up bowl) and stand them upside-down on kitchen paper to drain thoroughly before use.

PREPARING FRUIT & VEGETABLES

CITRUS FRUIT

If you're not too good at wielding a knife to cut citrus peel into neat strips for marmalade, try a pair of scissors instead. If you don't mind what the finished result looks like – zap the whole lot through the food processor!

To extract the maximum juice from citrus fruit, warm them up first. Microwave each one on full power for 15–30 seconds or cover with boiling water for a few minutes.

Some recipes call for citrus zest (sometimes also called rind): this is the thin, brightly coloured outer layer of citrus fruits, which is where the powerful smell and flavour is to be found. The zest can be removed in several ways.

If you need just a little zest, use a special tool called a zester, which removes the zest in shreds.

If you need to remove the zest in one long strip, use a potato peeler. Pared rind is sometimes used to infuse flavour into liquids and it is easier to remove at the end than grated zest would be.

If you need a lot of zest, use a grater. I have treated myself to one of the fairly new microplane graters, which really are very efficient and almost effortless to use. The grating surface is made up of minute blades, which make the job so easy, and they come in three different grating surfaces, from coarse through to fine. Now I don't mind grating several lemons at a time! You can buy them in good kitchenware shops.

SKINNING PEACHES

Place the peaches in a heatproof bowl and pour over enough boiling water to cover the fruit. Leave for 1 minute only and pour away the hot water. Cover with cold water and leave for a few minutes to cool. The skin should now peel away easily.

SKINNING TOMATOES

Use the same method as for skinning peaches. Alternatively, if you have a gas flame, place the tomato on to a fork and carefully twirl the tomato over the gas flame. The heat will quickly blister the tomato skin, making it easy to peel away.

TO REHYDRATE DRIED APRICOTS IN THE MICROWAVE

This saves having to wait overnight! Put 225 g (8 oz) of dried apricots in a dish and cover them with water. Cover and cook on full power for 4 minutes. Leave to stand for 3 minutes.

No-need-to-soak /ready-to-eat dried apricots can be used straight from the packet, without rehydration.

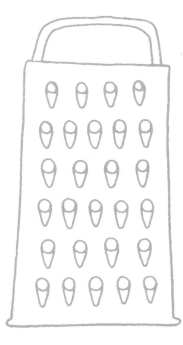

TIPS FOR SUCCESSFULLY COOKING PRESERVES

JELLIES

Scald the jelly bag or cloth with boiling water first – then the juice will run through and not be absorbed by the fabric.

You need patience to allow enough time for the jelly to drip through to extract the pulp. Trying to hurry it along by squeezing the bag will often give a cloudy result.

MARMALADES

Remember that you need to reduce the fruit mixture by at least a half before adding the sugar. To achieve this reduction, cover the fruit during the first stage of cooking, to get the peel really soft, and then cook uncovered to allow excess water to evaporate. Then you'll have the right level of concentrated pulp for a fantastic flavour and sufficient pectin for a good set.

To avoid having hard peel in the finished marmalade you must make sure that the fruit is very soft and squashy before adding the sugar. Test with a fork or cool a bit and eat it. If you're using different varieties of citrus fruit then test each one – they do vary.

Warming the sugar (below) before adding it to the fruit will help it to dissolve faster and setting point can be obtained more quickly.

If for some reason you don't achieve a good set, do not despair! Runny marmalade is excellent for sauces; in cakes and puddings and for a delicious baste for sausages and ham.

ADDING THE SUGAR

It's a good idea to warm the sugar first, either in a low oven or in the microwave for 1 minute on full power. This helps the sugar to dissolve more quickly.

Only add sugar when the fruit is completely tender and the contents of the pan has reduced by about half from the quantity you began with. If the sugar is added too soon, the boiling required to reduce the mixture to the right concentration will affect the finished colour and flavour, as well as the set.

The golden rule for jam-making is: slow cooking before the sugar is added and very rapid and short cooking afterwards.

ESSENTIALS FOR A GOOD SET

Jams, jellies and marmalades depend on the right combination of pectin, acid and sugar to achieve a good set. It would be great if all fruit contained equal amounts of pectin and acid and all we had to do was add the right amount of sugar! But real life is much more complicated than this. A preserve may react slightly differently every time you make it, even though you use the same recipe, because the fruit will contain more or less acid and pectin, according to the variety, freshness and degree of ripeness of the fruit, the season and the weather. A reliable recipe should help guarantee success.

Acid is important as it helps in the process of extracting the pectin from the fruit. It is essential for a good set, improves the flavour, brightens the colour and helps to prevent crystallisation of the sugar. Fruit rich in pectin (see page 20) is usually rich in acid also. Extra acidity is included in the recipe if low-acid fruits are used. This could be in the form of lemon juice, citric or tartaric acid, redcurrant, gooseberry or apple stock.

Sugar is not used just for its sweetness. The concentration of sugar in the finished preserve must be such that it prevents fermentation and crystallisation from occurring. How this happens and why it sometimes fails to happen is a matter of quite complex chemistry – making it all the more important to follow a reliable recipe. Further reading and explanations can be found in the HMSO publication Bulletin 21 *Home Preservation of Fruit and Vegetables*; this excellent publication was first published in 1929 by the then Ministry of Agriculture, Fisheries and Food and the fourteenth edition came out in 1989! (See page 80 for address.)

Pectin is a natural gum-like substance found in the cell walls of all plant food. Extracting it from the fruit is the first stage in making preserves. Pectin is best and most easily extracted from just-ripe and slightly under-ripe fruit. If the fruit is over-ripe, the pectin will not gel.

If you use a good, reliable recipe, it is rarely necessary to measure the pectin content of the fruit you are going to use. Where low-pectin fruit is used, it is usually blended with a high-pectin fruit to achieve the right balance. For example, a grated cooking apple to each 450 g (1 lb) of strawberries will produce a good set without spoiling the flavour.

Gooseberry Mint Jelly (page 39)

However, there is a very simple test to check the pectin content of the fruit pulp after simmering but before you add the sugar. This will give a good indication whether to add more pectin or whether to cook for a little longer to extract more pectin.

Take a teaspoon of juice from the pan, pour into a small glass container and allow it to cool. Add a tablespoon of methylated spirit to the cooled juice and shake well. After about a minute, a transparent clot should form.

If the clot is large and jelly-like, the pectin content is high. No extra pectin is needed.

If the clot is in two or three lumps, the pectin content is medium, but adequate for a set.

If there is no clot, or if there are lots of very small ones, the pectin content is low. Extra pectin is needed.

When you do a pectin test, move away from your jam pan. A friend of TV presenter Grace Mulligan ruined a batch of jam by inadvertently pouring the methylated spirit test clot back into the pan of jam!

If a pectin test shows a low pectin level, add about 50–100 ml (2–4 fl oz) of pectin stock for every 450 g (1 lb) fruit. If using a commercial liquid pectin, follow the manufacturer's instructions.

HIGH-PECTIN FRUIT:
Blackcurrants • Redcurrants • Damsons • Quinces • Cooking apples • Gooseberries • Some varieties of plum

MEDIUM-PECTIN FRUIT:
Raspberries • Early blackberries • Fresh apricots • Greengages • Loganberries

LOW-PECTIN FRUIT:
Strawberries • Pears • Elderberries • Cherries • Late blackberries

EXTRACTING THE PECTIN FROM CITRUS FRUITS FOR MARMALADE

This important procedure is usually done by placing all the pith and pips from the prepared fruit into a ready-made muslin bag or into a square of muslin which is then drawn up and tied into a bag with string. Don't draw up the bag too tightly; the water from the cooking of the fruit needs to be able to wash through the contents of the bag, thus extracting the pectin.

Muslin is usually sold off the roll in good kitchen shops or it can be obtained in squares or as ready-made bags.

Another method, which I prefer to use especially when making marmalade, when you could have quite a bulky amount of pith, is to put everything into a small saucepan. Cover with some of the cooking water and boil for 10 minutes. Rub through a sieve and place back in the pan for the final stage of boiling with the sugar (see Claire Macdonald's Citrus Fruit Marmalade, page 64).

TO MAKE YOUR OWN PECTIN STOCK

Don't throw away the peel, core and pips when preparing apples for your chutney or for pies. Cover with water and cook gently for 45 minutes to an hour. Pour the contents of the pan through a jelly bag and allow to drip through – the resulting liquid is virtually tasteless pectin stock. Test it to make sure you have a good pectin level and then freeze in 300 ml ('/2-pint) containers. It is then ready to add to any jam needing pectin and will preserve the true taste of the fruit being used.

Use this method for redcurrants and gooseberries. Or add one grated cooking apple for every 900 g (2 lb) of fruit

Pectin can also be bought commercially and is commonly used in the no-cook freezer jams.

TESTING FOR A SET

There are three simple ways of testing whether a jam, jelly or marmalade has reached setting point. It is important to keep the preserve off the heat during the test or it may go beyond the point of setting. I usually use the flake and saucer tests together. The flake test is a good indicator and the saucer test will confirm.

FLAKE TEST

Dip a clean wooden spoon into the jam. Remove it and, holding it above the pan, twirl the spoon a few times to cool the jam. Let the jam fall off the spoon. If the drops run together and form flakes that 'hang' on the edge of the spoon, a setting point has been achieved.

COLD SAUCER TEST

Chill a plate in the refrigerator. Put a teaspoon of jam on to the plate and let it cool for 1 minute. Push the surface of the jam: if it wrinkles, the jam has reached setting point.

THERMOMETER TEST

Stir the jam. Dip the thermometer into hot water before dipping into the jam. If the temperature reaches 105°C/220°F, setting point should have been reached.

REMOVING SCUM

Some froth or scum may appear on the surface of the preserve as it cooks; this is simply the result of air bubbles forming in the preserve and the movement of ingredients. It is not harmful but doesn't look very nice in the finished preserve. The amount varies greatly; some recipes may not form any at all. Don't try to remove scum while the preserve is cooking, as this can be wasteful; wait until setting point has been reached but don't let the preserve cool. The simplest way to disperse small amounts of scum is to add a knob of butter to the finished preserve as soon as it is taken off the heat. Larger amounts can be removed by skimming the surface of the preserve with a spoon and then any traces dealt with by a knob of butter. Some recipes suggest rubbing the pan with a small knob of butter before cooking.

POTTING
(PUTTING THE FINISHED PRESERVE INTO STERILISED JARS)

Be ready!
Have your jars sterilised and cooled (see page 16).
    Have your covers ready-matched to fit the jars (see page 14).
    Organise a production line – it really works.
    You need to find a system with which you are comfortable. The process needs to be safe but fairly speedy as the covers need to be applied while the preserve is still hot. I was taught by a WI Market colleague, Janet Morgan, to pot into cooled jars – not hot as most books will tell you. I find that a most dangerous practice, as you need to hold the jar firmly and not through an oven glove or mitt. I have never had an accident with the jar shattering but I always hold the jar I am filling over a plate and not the pan of preserve. You can easily hold the cooled jar as you fill it right to the brim with the hot preserve and apply the cover before the jar gets too hot to handle.
    I use a small stainless steel measuring jug to 'ladle' the preserve into the jar – pouring straight in without a funnel or any other device. I have a brand new and wetted J cloth to hand to wipe any drips straightaway.
    It is important in our home kitchens to fill jars absolutely to the brim and apply the cover straight away. This eliminates the possibility of airborne bacteria getting in and spoiling the preserve. The head-space we see in commercial brands is achieved in rather different surroundings to those we have in our kitchens. So better to be safe than sorry and have to throw out a jam that turns out to be mouldy when you come to use it.

STORAGE

Most preserves, that is, jams, jellies, marmalades, chutneys and pickles, if they are made with the correct proportion of sugar or vinegar and put in properly sterilised and sealed containers, will keep for up to a year (and some for considerably longer), given good conditions. The storage place needs to be cool, dark and dry. Too much heat will make the contents shrink. Too much light may fade the colour. Damp may cause moulds to grow on the surface of the preserve. Many modern homes lack sufficient suitable storage space so you may need to commission a cupboard in the garage or other outhouse. Otherwise you will have to store them in the fridge.

Once opened, preserves are subject to contamination by airborne bacteria, so the contents need to be eaten within 3–4 weeks and may be best kept in the fridge.

EXCEPTIONS TO THESE GENERAL GUIDELINES ARE THE FOLLOWING:

FRUIT CURDS: Store in the fridge for up to six weeks. Once opened, store in the fridge and use within 3–4 weeks.

LOW-SUGAR JAMS: Store for up to six months. Once opened, store in the fridge and use within 2–3 weeks.

UNCOOKED CHUTNEYS & RELISHES: Store for up to six months. Once opened, store in the fridge and use within 2–3 weeks.

Check opened jars regularly for any change in colour, signs of mould or deterioration or any unpleasant smell. If necessary, discard immediately.

APPLYING COVERS

Twist tops must be applied as soon as the preserve is ready and potted. Fill the jar to the brim. As the preserve cools it shrinks and forms a vacuum.

Waxed discs must also be applied immediately in order to melt the wax, which in turn forms a seal. Therefore it is essential that the disc fits the neck of the jar. The cellophane cover can be applied when the preserve is hot or cold and is simply a dust cover.

LABELLING & PRESENTATION

It is important to label your preserves as soon as possible after the jars have cooled down and set. No matter how good your memory is – you will forget what's in unlabelled jars. Remember, you may not be using the preserve for some time and several batches into the year you will have forgotten what a particular batch was and which recipe you used. Label each jar with the type of preserve and the date of making; it is also useful to add a note of the book the recipe came from.

Most stationers and kitchen shops sell matching labels and decorative covers, which give an attractive finish to your preserves.

Use some pretty material or wrapping paper to make tops for your preserves, add a fancy label and you'll never be short of a home-made gift or contribution to the local fund-raising efforts. Most people can't or don't want to make their own preserves and are more than happy to buy someone else's.

From the top: Passion Fruit Curd, Lemon Curd Ice Cream, Lemon Curd (all page 24)

SPRING PRESERVES

MAKES: about 1.3 kg (3 lb)
PREPARATION TIME: 15 minutes
COOKING TIME: about 10 minutes in
microwave; otherwise, 40 minutes

200 g (7 oz) butter, preferably unsalted
700 g (1 lb 9 oz) granulated or caster sugar
grated zest of 4–5 lemons
300 ml ('/2 pint) lemon juice
(about 4–5 lemons)
300 ml ('/2 pint) beaten eggs
(about 4–5 eggs)

The beauty of this classic recipe for lemon curd is that the eggs and the lemon juice are measured and therefore you get a consistent result whatever the size of eggs or juice content of the lemons. **I love eating it whether on my breakfast toast or as a filling for a pudding or in a deliciously simple ice cream** which came from Glenys Gibson. It has now become Nan's Ice Cream as my granddaughter, Isabel, seems to have inherited a taste for it too. The lemon curd recipe is from the HMSO Bulletin 21 publication, to which I was first introduced at college in 1963.

I cook this in the microwave, which only takes about 10 minutes, compared with about 40 minutes in a double-boiler or in a bowl over a pan of hot water. I sometimes use up to four egg yolks in the measured egg, making up the rest of the amount with whole eggs.

LEMON CURD *pictured on page 23*

1 Place the butter, sugar, lemon zest and juice in a large bowl and microwave on full power for about 2 minutes or until the butter has melted and the sugar has dissolved. (Or use the top of a double-boiler or a bowl over a pan of hot water.)
2 Add the beaten eggs and continue cooking in 1-minute bursts and stirring each time, reducing to 30 seconds for each burst as the mixture thickens, until the mixture is thick enough to coat the back of the spoon.
3 Strain through a sieve into a wide-necked jug, to remove the lemon zest and any cooked egg bits. Put into cooled, sterilised jars and cover with a waxed disc and cellophane (see pages 16 and 22). Label and store in the refrigerator.

PASSION FRUIT CURD: Add the seeds and pulp of four ripe passion fruit just before potting.

ELDERFLOWER CURD: Carefully strip the tiny flowers from the stems of 2–3 handfuls of elderflowers and add to the curd when cooking.

SERVING IDEAS: Use to fill a meringue pavlova or roulade, with whipped cream or half and half cream and Greek-style yoghurt.

Serve folded through Greek-style yoghurt or a thick natural yoghurt.

Use to fill a freshly baked sandwich cake or Swiss roll

LEMON CURD ICE CREAM

450 g (1 lb) jar of lemon curd
grated zest and juice of 1 lemon
300 ml ('/2 pint) whipping cream
450 g (1 lb) Greek-style yoghurt

1 Use a long loaf tin, lined with cling film, or a plastic container.
2 Beat the zest and juice into the curd.
3 Add the cream and yoghurt and stir until smooth.
4 Pour the mixture into the tin and freeze for 4–6 hours or until firm.
5 Remove from the freezer to refrigerator about 1 hour before serving. Remove from tin and cut into slices.

NOTE: The ice cream can be kept for up to 3 months.

This is a good example of how names change as they are handed on. When teaching at Denman College I always include a Recipe Swapshop for the students to bring along and share their favourite recipes. This recipe was brought along to a 'Preserves' course by Dawn Taylor from the Lincolnshire South Federation. I rang Dawn to check with her where the recipe originated, as I couldn't quite make out why it should be called '**Easter**' Chutney. Dawn said she'd been given the recipe by a lady in her village and on checking the recipe found that she'd missed out an 'n' – making it 'Eastern' Chutney – hence the oranges and dates!

MAKES: about 1.8 kg (4 lb)
PREPARATION & COOKING TIME:
about 1 hour

EASTER CHUTNEY

450 g (1 lb) oranges (3–4 medium-size)
450 g (1 lb) onions, chopped
450 g (1 lb) stoned dates
225 g (8 oz) sultanas
675 g (1½ lb) demerara sugar
2 teaspoons salt
½ teaspoon cayenne pepper
575 ml (1 pint) malt vinegar

1 Remove the zest of 1 orange using a potato peeler and leave to one side.
2 Peel all the oranges, removing as much pith as possible. Chop the fruit roughly and discard the pips and the peel (or pop it in a bag in the freezer to make marmalade later).
3 Coarsely mince (or use a food processor to shred) the onions, dates, orange flesh and reserved orange zest and put on a plate.

4 Put the sultanas, sugar, salt, cayenne pepper and vinegar into a preserving pan. Bring the mixture to the boil and add the minced/shredded mixture.
5 Return to the boil and then reduce the heat and simmer until the chutney is thick and free of liquid – about 30 minutes.
6 Spoon the chutney into cooled, sterilised jars and cover with vinegar-proof lids (see pages 16 and 22). Label and store for 6–8 weeks before use.

MAKES: about 2.2 kg (5 lb)
PREPARATION & COOKING TIME:
overnight standing + 1 hour cooking + 40 minutes

RHUBARB & ORANGE JAM *pictured opposite, left*

This is one of the first jams ever made by Ann Creasey, our WI Markets Adviser in Lincolnshire North. Ann remembers her first attempt, when she thought the jam was going to set in the pan. They consequently had some tasty but rather stretchy rhubarb sweets! Ann has made lots more since then and now feels it is just about the easiest and a most delicious jam to make. It looks great, too, and would make an ideal addition to a Christmas hamper.

1.3 kg (3 lb) rhubarb, cut into 2.5 cm (1-inch) lengths
1.3 kg (3 lb) granulated sugar
grated zest and juice of 1 lemon
2 thin-skinned oranges

1 Put alternate layers of rhubarb and sugar into a non-metallic bowl. Add the lemon zest and juice. Cover and leave for 24 hours.
2 Next day, boil the oranges in 575 ml (1 pint) of water for about 1 hour or until translucent.
3 Cut five thin slices from the oranges and then chop the remaining orange, discarding any pips.
4 Place the rhubarb and sugar mixture with the chopped oranges into a large preserving pan and bring slowly to the boil, stirring until the sugar has dissolved.
5 Boil rapidly until setting point is reached (see page 21), stirring only occasionally. Cool slightly and remove any scum (see page 21). Stir again.
6 Fill each sterilised jar a quarter full and then slide an orange slice down the side of each jar. Fill to the brim carefully, without disturbing the orange slice. Cover and label on the side opposite the orange slice. (See pages 16 and 22 for information on sterilising jars and sealing the filled jars.)

RHUBARB, ORANGE & GINGER JAM: Add 50–80 g (2–3 oz) finely chopped stem ginger preserved in syrup or crystallised ginger.

MAKES: about 2.2 kg (5 lb)
PREPARATION & COOKING TIME:
overnight standing + 55 minutes

RHUBARB & FIG JAM *pictured opposite, right*

Judith Wilson of Tealby WI is our local WI Adviser and treasured Treasurer of Market Rasen & District WI Market. Judith's mother used to make this jam regularly and it was Judith's favourite as a child. Judith says she hasn't come across the recipe anywhere else nor heard of anyone else who makes it. The jam is very similar to Rhubarb and Orange Jam (opposite), a recipe from Ann Creasey.

1.3 kg (3 lb) rhubarb, cut into 2.5 cm (1-inch) pieces
1.3 kg (3 lb) granulated sugar
225 g (8 oz) dried figs, chopped
juice of 3 lemons

1 Place the rhubarb in a large bowl (not metal) and cover with the sugar. Leave overnight.
2 Next day, place the rhubarb, sugar, figs and lemon juice in a large preserving pan. Heat gently until the sugar has dissolved.
3 Bring to the boil and boil until setting point is reached (see page 21) – about 30 minutes. Remove any scum (see page 21).
4 Ladle into cooled, sterilised jars and seal (see pages 16 and 22).

RHUBARB, ORANGE & CANDIED PEEL JAM: Add finely chopped candied peel to the rhubarb and sugar before leaving overnight. Allow 40 g (1½ oz) of peel per 450 g (1 lb) of rhubarb.

RHUBARB & BLACKCURRANT JAM

MAKES: about 2.2 kg (5 lb)
PREPARATION & COOKING TIME:
1 hour

I devised this delicious combination of fruits when I started teaching cookery at Denman College on the WI Markets courses, the first of which was always in May. I used rhubarb from the garden and blackcurrants from the freezer from the previous year.

900 g (2 lb) blackcurrants, washed
  and stalks removed
675 g (1 1/2 lb) rhubarb, washed and sliced
1.5 kg (3 lb 5 oz) sugar

1 Place the fruit and 425 ml (15 fl oz) of water in a large preserving pan. Bring to the boil and then gently simmer until the fruit is quite soft – about 20 minutes. Remove from the heat.
2 Add the sugar and stir until dissolved.
3 Return to the heat and bring to the boil. Boil rapidly until setting point is reached (see page 21). Remove any scum (see page 21). Test for a set after 5–10 minutes.
4 Pour into cooled, sterilised jars, seal and label (see pages 16 and 22).

RHUBARB & DATE CHUTNEY

MAKES: about three 450 g (1 lb) jars
PREPARATION TIME: about 20 minutes
COOKING TIME: 1–2 hours

This is a recipe I've had written in my recipe book for some time but, for whatever reason, I haven't added the usual note of from where or from whom it came. It's a good one to make earlier in the year rather than during the usual chutney season in the autumn. It is particularly delicious in a strong-flavoured cheese sandwich or with cold meats.

900 g (2 lb) rhubarb, trimmed and cut into 5 cm (2-inch) chunks
450 g (1 lb) onions, chopped roughly
115 g (4 oz) dates, chopped
300 ml (1/2 pint) each of malt vinegar and water
450 g (1 lb) granulated or demerara sugar
1 level tablespoon salt
1 level tablespoon ground ginger
1/2 teaspoon cayenne pepper

1 Place all the ingredients in a large saucepan and bring to the boil. Reduce the heat and simmer gently until the chutney has a jam-like consistency and there is no excess liquid on the surface. Stir from time to time to prevent sticking.
2 Allow to cool slightly.
3 Spoon into cooled, sterilised jars and seal with vinegar-proof tops (see pages 16 and 22). Label and store for 6–8 weeks before use.

RHUBARB & GARLIC CHUTNEY: Add 2 crushed cloves of garlic and the zest of 1 orange and 1 lemon.

RHUBARB & GINGER CHUTNEY: Omit the dates and add 50 g (2 oz) of finely chopped stem ginger preserved in syrup or crystallised ginger.

RHUBARB & APRICOT, RAISIN OR SULTANA CHUTNEY: Replace the dates with chopped dried apricots or with raisins or sultanas.

Left: Ratatouille Chutney; right: Nectarine Chutney (both page 30); in the spoon: Brandied Grape & Apricot Jam (page 31)

SUMMER PRESERVES

MAKES: about enough to fill four 450 g (1 lb) jars
PREPARATION TIME: about 45 minutes
COOKING TIME: about 2–2½ hours

RATATOUILLE CHUTNEY *pictured on page 29*

This is one of my favourite chutney recipes. I once took a jar as a gift to one of the presenters of our WI Federation slot on BBC Radio Lincolnshire, Veronica Capaldi, which she duly took home and presented to her husband. The next time I saw Veronica she told me that her husband had spread spoonfuls on to grilled pork chops for the last few minutes cooking time – delicious. This is a strong and hot chutney.

900 g (2 lb) tomatoes, skinned and chopped
450 g (1 lb) spanish onions, chopped
450 g (1 lb) courgettes, sliced thinly
1 large green pepper, sliced
1 large red pepper, sliced
1 aubergine, diced
2 large garlic cloves, crushed
1 tablespoon salt
1 tablespoon cayenne pepper
1 tablespoon paprika
1 tablespoon ground coriander
300 ml (½ pint) malt vinegar
350 g (12 oz) granulated sugar

1 Place the tomatoes, onions, courgettes, peppers, aubergine and garlic in a large pan. Add the salt, cayenne and paprika and coriander. Cover and cook gently, stirring occasionally, until the juices run.
2 Bring to the boil, reduce the heat, uncover and simmer for 1–1½ hours or until the vegetables are soft but still recognisable as shapes, and most of the water from the tomatoes has evaporated.
3 Add the vinegar and sugar, stirring to dissolve the sugar. Continue to cook for 1 hour or until the chutney is thick and there is no free vinegar on top.
4 Spoon while still hot into cooled, sterilised jars and seal with vinegar-proof covers (see pages 16 and 22). Label and store for at least 2 months to mature

MAKES: about 1.3 kg (3 lb)
PREPARATION TIME: 30 minutes
COOKING TIME: about 1¾ hours

NECTARINE CHUTNEY *pictured on page 29*

I brought this recipe back from my cousin Wendy's in New Zealand as I love nectarines and was interested that it is cooked in the oven. I have since learned that it was quite common to cook chutneys in this way but I'd never come across such a recipe before. I love cooking Sunday lunch for family and friends and this was served with roast lamb only two weeks after making and was heartily approved. It is quite strongly flavoured with rosemary, so you could reduce the amount by up to a half. The recipe states that it can be made with any fruit.

1.1 kg (2¼ lb) nectarines, about 12 fruits, stoned and quartered
675 g (1½ lb) red onions, sliced finely
4 garlic cloves, chopped roughly
1 lemon, halved and pips removed, sliced finely
2 tablespoons chopped fresh rosemary
1 teaspoon cumin seeds
1 teaspoon fennel seeds
250 ml (9 fl oz) cider vinegar
500 g (1 lb 2 oz) demerara sugar

1 Preheat the oven to Gas Mark 6/electric oven 200°C/fan oven 180°C.
2 Put all the ingredients except the sugar into a large roasting tin. Mix well and roast for 1¼ hours, stirring occasionally.
3 When the mixture starts to reduce and colour, add the sugar. Cook for a further 30 minutes, stirring twice during this period. The chutney should be fairly dry and any liquid should be quite syrupy and jam-like. The shapes of the fruit should still be discernible.
4 Spoon into cooled, sterilised jars and cover with vinegar-proof lids (see pages 16 and 22). Label and store. This could be used straightaway but the flavour will mature on keeping.

MAKES: about 1.3 kg (3 lb)
PREPARATION TIME: 20 minutes + 2–3 hours standing
COOKING TIME: about 40 minutes

BRANDIED GRAPE & APRICOT JAM *pictured on page 29*

This recipe is from the very first book that I helped to edit. It was produced to celebrate the formation of our new Federation of Lincolnshire North in 1977, following the change in county boundaries. I have never got around to making it until recently and now I know what I've missed all these years – it is lovely. It was submitted by my longstanding friend, Joan Brown, stalwart of Scotton and District WI and of Gainsborough and District WI Market, and was a prizewinner in the Lincolnshire Show around that time. She suggests that it is delicious served with cold meats and that peaches can be used instead of apricots. The only alteration I have made is that I've added the brandy just before potting rather than at the beginning, to preserve its flavour in the finished jam.

I recently found a similar recipe which suggested that jams like these, with grapes, lemon, nuts and brandy, are part of the traditional Middle-Eastern welcoming ceremony, eaten with a spoon and accompanied by a glass of cold water.

225 g (8 oz) black grapes, halved and pips removed
225 g (8 oz) green grapes, halved and pips removed (or use 450 g/1 lb seedless grapes, halved, instead of both black and green grapes)
450 g (1 lb) apricots, halved and stoned
900 g (2 lb) granulated sugar
juice of 1 lemon
50 g (2 oz) blanched almonds, chopped (optional)
5 tablespoons brandy

1   Place the fruit in a preserving pan, with the sugar. Leave to stand for 2–3 hours.
2   Slowly bring to the boil, stirring until the sugar is dissolved.
3   Add the lemon juice and then boil rapidly until setting point is reached (see page 21). Remove any scum (see page 21). Add the almonds, if using, and the brandy.
4   Pour into cooled, sterilised jars and seal (see pages 16 and 22). Label and store.

NOTE: Apricot and almond is a favourite combination but other nuts can be added to jam: how about walnuts with plum jam? Or stir toasted pine kernels into raspberry jam.

MAKES: about 1.3 kg (3 lb)
PREPARATION TIME: 40 minutes
COOKING TIME: 45 minutes

PEACH MARMALADE

This preserve was served to Doreen Hancock of Willingham-by-Stow WI for breakfast with croissants on a twinning trip to France. Her hostess very kindly gave her the recipe. It is a lovely colour and tastes great. The ratio of sugar to fruit is not in the usual proportion and this makes the preserve unsuitable for long keeping (see page 22).

2 oranges, chopped (or sliced, if you prefer larger pieces of peel)
800 g (1³/₄ lb) sugar
115 ml (4 fl oz) water
1.3 kg (3 lb) peaches, skinned and chopped
juice of 1 lemon

1   In a large pan, cook the oranges with 200 g (7 oz) of the sugar and the water, until they are soft.
2   Add the peaches, with the rest of the sugar and the lemon juice. Stir until the sugar is dissolved and then bring to the boil.
3   Cook to setting point – about 15 minutes (see page 21). Remove any scum (see page 21).
4   Pour immediately into cooled, sterilised jars and seal (see pages 16 and 22). Label and store in a cool and dry place for up to 6 months. Once opened, store in the fridge and use within 3–4 weeks.

TRADITIONAL RASPBERRY JAM *pictured opposite and on page 7*

MAKES: about 2.2 kg (5 lb)
PREPARATION & COOKING TIME:
40 minutes

**1.3 kg (3 lb) raspberries, washed and
drained well if necessary
1.3 kg (3 lb) granulated sugar**

This must be one of the all-time favourites and so easy to make. It can be rather expensive if you have to buy the fruit, which is why I have included some variations with some less expensive partners. The nectarine version is a particular favourite of mine and Christine Sherriff sent me the peach one, which, of course, is very similar. They all have a beautiful aroma and the taste is delectable. Use to fill a freshly-made sponge cake or team it up with fromage frais or flavoured mascarpone cheese for a special teatime treat or party pudding.

1   Place the raspberries in a large pan and simmer gently for about 10 minutes, until the raspberries are tender and the juice is extracted.
2   Remove from the heat and add the sugar, stirring until it is completely dissolved.
3   Put the pan back on the heat and bring to the boil. Boil rapidly for about 5 minutes and then remove any scum (see page 21). and test for a set (see page 21).
4   Pour into cooled, sterilised jars and then seal and label (see pages 16 and 22).

RASPBERRY & NECTARINE (OR PEACH) JAM: Replace half of the raspberries with 675 g (1½ lb) chopped nectarines or peeled peaches and add 150 ml (¼ pint) of water and 2 tablespoons of lemon juice. Cook the nectarines or peaches first with the water and lemon juice until soft – about 5 minutes. Add the raspberries and simmer for a further 5 minutes. Continue as above.

RASPBERRY & RHUBARB JAM: Again, replace half the raspberries with rhubarb and add 150 ml (¼ pint) of water. Cook for about 15 minutes before adding the raspberries. Continue as above.

APRICOT & HONEY CONSERVE

MAKES: about 450 g (1 lb)
PREPARATION TIME: 10 minutes

**225 g (8 oz) honey
225 g (8 oz) apricots
4 teaspoons lemon juice
½ teaspoon ground cinnamon
2 tablespoons brandy**

This is a very quick and easy recipe from *Simply Good Food*, a book published by the NFWI Wales following their 'Lose Weight Wales' campaign 10 years ago. About 2,500 individual WI members and their families became fitter and healthier through following the campaign and the cookbook was devised to help them achieve their aims.

1   Process all the ingredients together. Store in a sterilised (see page 16) jar with an airtight top for up to 6 months. Once opened, use within 2–3 weeks.

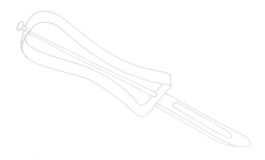

MAKES: about 1.1 kg (2¼ lb)
PREPARATION & COOKING TIME: about 50 minutes

This quick microwave version of strawberry jam is delicious. You can't really taste the apple – the strawberry flavour shines through.

MICROWAVE STRAWBERRY JAM WITH APPLE

115 g (4 oz) prepared weight peeled and
   chopped cooking apple
675 g (1½ lb) strawberries
675 g (1½ lb) granulated sugar

1 Place the apples in a large bowl. Cover with cling film and puncture a couple of times. Cook on full power for 5 minutes. Remove the cover and mash the apple.
2 Add the strawberries and stir. Cook on full power for 5 minutes and then stir and mash the fruit. Cook on full power for a further 10 minutes.
3 Add the sugar and stir to dissolve. Continue to cook for 2 minutes on full and stir well. Remove any scum (see page 21).
4 Cook for 3 minutes and test for a set (see page 21). Continue cooking for 1 minute and testing in the intervals, if necessary, until setting point is reached.
5 Pour into cooled, sterilised jars, seal and label (see pages 16 and 22).

MAKES: 1.1 litres (2 pints)
PREPARATION TIME: 15 minutes + 3–6 days standing
COOKING TIME: 20 minutes

Fruit vinegars are very easy to make, even if you do have to wait a few days for the initial stage to be completed. The unsweetened vinegar can be used in salad dressings, sauces or drinks. The sweetened version is an excellent remedy for a sore throat (taken neat and hot) and can be used to make summer drinks, or pour it on freshly-made pancakes for one of the best puddings ever. You can also use blackberries, gooseberries (chopped roughly), blueberries, or blackcurrants. I have also made this with strawberries and with a mixture of berries.

RASPBERRY VINEGAR

450 g (1 lb) raspberries, washed only if absolutely necessary
   and then drained well
575 ml (1 pint) wine or cider vinegar
sugar (see step 3)

1 Place the fruit in a glass, china or earthenware bowl and pour the vinegar over it. Cover the bowl with a cloth and leave to stand in a cool place for 4–6 days, stirring each day. I usually pop a plate over the top to save anyone inadvertently placing anything on it.
2 Strain off and measure the liquid. For the unsweetened version, strain the vinegar through a jelly bag or filter. Pour into sterilised (page 16) bottles and seal.
3 For the sweetened version, weigh 450 g (1 lb) of sugar for each 575 ml (1 pint) of vinegar. Put the liquid into a large pan and heat gently. Add the sugar and stir until it is completely dissolved. Bring to the boil and boil for 10 minutes. Pour into sterilised bottles and cork or seal with screw top. Leave to mature for at least 2 weeks before using.

MAKES: about 2 kg (4¹/₂ lb)
PREPARATION TIME: I hour
COOKING TIME; 45 minutes

Gill Worrell, of Marton WI and
Gainsborough WI Market, sent me this
recipe. Gill quickens up the process by
cooking the gooseberries and onions in the
microwave first, which will obviously reduce
the total cooking time considerably. Gill
always uses sultanas rather than raisins and
the lighter brown sugar. Gill also makes the
chutney with red gooseberries, which
produce a good colour. You could substitute
tarragon vinegar for half the malt vinegar, for
a different flavour.

GOOSEBERRY CHUTNEY

1.3 kg (3 lb) gooseberries
225 g (8 oz) onions
225 g (8 oz) sultanas
20 g (³/₄ oz) salt, or less if preferred
450 g (I lb) sugar
850 ml (I¹/₂ pints) malt vinegar
I tablespoon allspice berries
I tablespoon ground ginger
¹/₄ teaspoon cayenne pepper

1 Place all the ingredients in a large
   preserving pan. Bring to the boil and
   then reduce the heat and simmer,
   uncovered, until the chutney is of a thick
   and pulpy consistency, about 45 minutes.
2 Spoon into cooled, sterilised jars and seal
   with a vinegar-proof cover (see pages 16
   and 22). Label and store for at least 4–6
   weeks before using.

MAKES: about 1.4 kg (3 lb)
PREPARATION TIME: 20 minutes
COOKING TIME:
30 minutes in microwave; otherwise, I hour

Gooseberries make a lovely tangy curd.
Some people prefer to keep in the skins and
seeds of the fruit but I prefer a smooth curd.
If you're not going to sieve it, though, you
need to top and tail the fruit.

900 g (2 lb) gooseberries
450 g (I lb) granulated sugar
115 g (4 oz) butter, preferably unsalted
4 eggs, beaten

GOOSEBERRY CURD

1 Place the gooseberries and 2–3 tablespoons of water in a large bowl and
   cover with pierced cling film. Microwave
   on full power for 10–15 minutes or until
   very soft. Rub through a sieve to remove
   skins and seeds.
2 Return to the bowl and add the sugar
   and butter. Cook on full power for 2
   minutes or until the butter is melted and
   the sugar is dissolved.
3 Add the eggs and stir well. Cook, stirring
   frequently, until the mixture is thick and
   will coat the back of a spoon.
4 I prefer to strain this again, to remove any
   bits of cooked egg. Pour into cooled,
   sterilised jars and seal with a waxed disc
   (see pages 16 and 22). Cover with cellophane and store in the fridge for up to 6
   weeks. Once opened, use within 2 weeks.

MAKES: 575 ml (I pint)
PREPARATION TIME: 10 minutes
COOKING TIME:
10 minutes + allow 24 hours infusion

An old college friend, Sue, sent me this
recipe, which she uses as a drink with
sparkling mineral water. It keeps well in the
fridge for several months but I can't see it
lasting that long. Sue also uses it in her
baked gooseberry and elderflower cheese-
cake, which is a favourite with the family
and at work.

ELDERFLOWER CORDIAL

6–8 elderflowers
575 ml (I pint) water
450 g (I lb) caster sugar
2 teaspoons citric acid or cider vinegar
juice and grated zest of I lemon

1 Bring the sugar and water gently to the
   boil and stir until the sugar is dissolved.
2 Put the elderflowers in a bowl and pour
   the sugar solution over them. Stir in the
   citric acid or cider vinegar, the lemon
   juice and zest. Cover and leave for 24
   hours to infuse.
3 Strain through muslin and bottle into
   sterilised (see pages 16 and 22)
   containers

TRADITIONAL STRAWBERRY JAM

MAKES: 2.2 kg (5 lb)
PREPARATION & COOKING TIME: about 45 minutes

Strawberry jam is another sure winner when it comes to flavour and is so evocative of our British summer. The art of making it really depends on how you like your strawberries in the finished jam, which is why there seem to be so many different versions around.

Mashing the fruit helps to release the pectin, thereby ensuring a good set. A strawberry jam can be notoriously difficult to set, no matter how diligent you are in selecting the right fruit, adding the acid and so on, so you might need to add extra pectin. Don't let it put you off having a go – it'll taste great.

1.3 kg (3 lb) strawberries, hulled and wiped,
  washed if necessary and drained really well
juice of 1 large lemon (about 2 tablespoons)
1.3 kg (3 lb) granulated sugar

1 Put the fruit in a large pan with the lemon juice and simmer gently until the juices begin to run – about 10 minutes.
2 Mash the strawberries down with a potato masher and continue to simmer for another 5 minutes, until the fruit is reduced to a thick purée.
3 Remove from the heat and carry out a pectin test (see page 20) and, if necessary, add pectin stock or a commercial pectin.
4 Add the sugar and stir until it is completely dissolved. Bring to the boil and boil for about 5 minutes before removing any scum (see page 21) and testing for a set (see page 21). If necessary, boil for longer and test again.
5 Pour into cooled, sterilised jars and seal (see pages 16 and 22). Label and store.

STRAWBERRY & ELDERFLOWER JAM: Add 3–4 handfuls of elderflowers to the strawberries.

STRAWBERRY & LEMONGRASS JAM: Add 4 lemongrass stalks, which have been lightly flattened with a rolling pin, to the strawberries as they cook. Remove stalks before potting the jam.

STRAWBERRY JAM WITH LIQUEUR: As above but add 2 teaspoons of liqueur (such as Grand Marnier or Cointreau) to each jar before pouring in the hot jam.

STRAWBERRY & GOOSEBERRY (OR RHUBARB) JAM: Replace half of the strawberries with topped and tailed gooseberries or chopped rhubarb and add 150 ml (¼ pint) of water. Cook the gooseberries or rhubarb in the water until they are quite tender – about 15 minutes. Add the strawberries and continue to simmer for about 5 minutes. Continue as main recipe.

STRAWBERRY & REDCURRANT JAM: Use 900 g (2 lb) of strawberries and 450 g (1 lb) of redcurrants, removed from stem, and add 575 ml (1 pint) of water. Simmer the redcurrants in the water until soft and then add the strawberries. Finish as main recipe.

STRAWBERRY & PASSION FRUIT JAM: Make the jam as the main recipe and add the pulp of four passion fruits to the finished jam.

STRAWBERRY CONSERVE

MAKES: 2.2 kg (5 lb)
PREPARATION & COOKING TIME:
24 hours standing + about 45 minutes + 48 hours standing

This is very similar to the main recipe but the resulting set is much softer and the fruits remain whole and suspended.

1 Place the whole strawberries in a bowl with alternate layers of sugar. Cover and leave for 24 hours.
2 Next day, tip the contents of the bowl into a large preserving pan and bring to the boil, stirring occasionally. Boil for 5 minutes and then tip the contents back into the bowl. Cover and leave for 48 hours.
3 Return the fruit to the pan and bring to the boil. Boil for 10–15 minutes until setting point is reached (page 21). Remove any scum (see page 21). Cool until a skin starts to form.
4 Stir to distribute the fruit and then pot into cooled, sterilised (pages 16 and 22) jars.

MAKES: about 2.7 kg (6 lb)
PREPARATION TIME: 30 minutes
COOKING TIME: 40 minutes

MAKES about 1.5 kg (3 lb 5 oz)
PREPARATION TIME: 30 minutes
COOKING TIME: about 2 hours

TUTTI FRUTTI JAM

SOUTH SEAS CHUTNEY

This is a favourite of mine and very fruity, as the name suggests. I first made it from a WI Home Skills book written by Olive Odell in the late seventies. I have seen several variations of it with different names, such as 'Midsummer Jam', and 'Four-Fruit Jam' (see below). The success of the jam is in the combination of high, medium and low pectin content of the different fruit. Make sure you cook the currants until they are really soft as, once the sugar is added, you're at the point of no return! The best way to strip the currants from the stem is to hold the stalk in one hand and use a fork to slide down the stem and strip away the fruit.

450 g (1 lb) blackcurrants, stripped from stalks
450 g (1 lb) redcurrants, stripped from stalks
450 g (1 lb) strawberries, hulled
450 g (1 lb) raspberries, hulled
1.8 kg (4 lb) granulated sugar

1 Place the blackcurrants and redcurrants in a large preserving pan with 150 ml (¼ pint) of water. Bring to the boil and then gently simmer for about 15–20 minutes, ensuring that the skins of the currants are soft.
2 Add the strawberries and raspberries and simmer for a further 10 minutes.
3 Add the sugar, stirring until dissolved. Bring to the boil and boil rapidly until setting point is reached (see page 21).
4 Remove any scum from surface of jam, if necessary (page 21). Pour into cooled, sterilised jars and seal (see pages 16 and 22). Label and store.

MIDSUMMER JAM: Replace the blackcurrants with gooseberries.

FOUR-FRUIT JAM: Replace the redcurrants with gooseberries.

This was Sue Prickett's entry in the WI Country Markets Millennium Preserve Competition and it came top in Cumbria Westmorland. Sue reckons ripe mangoes are the best choice as they break down more easily. The raspberry vinegar and the lime juice add that indefinable something which is the key to the different and exotic taste.

450 g (1 lb) onions, chopped
300 ml (½ pint) raspberry vinegar
300 ml (½ pint) white-wine vinegar
3 mangoes, peeled and chopped
432 g can of crushed pineapple in juice
1 tablespoon grated fresh root ginger
3 teaspoons ground ginger
2 teaspoons ground coriander
1 teaspoons ground cumin
½ teaspoon ground cloves
½ teaspoon ground allspice
2 teaspoons lime juice
50 g (2 oz) sultanas
450 g (1 lb) golden granulated sugar
25 g (1 oz) flaked almonds

1 Gently cook the onion in the vinegars for 5 minutes. Add the mangoes, pineapple with juice, ginger, spices and lime juice and cook until soft – about 40 minutes to 1 hour.
2 Add the sultanas and salt and cook for a further 15 minutes.
3 Add the sugar and cook until reduced and there is no free vinegar. Add the almonds.
4 Spoon into cooled, sterilised jars, seal and label (see pages 16 and 22). Store for 6–8 weeks before using.

MAKES: about 1.1 kg (2¼ lb)
PREPARATION & COOKING TIME:
1–1½ hours + draining overnight

GOOSEBERRY MINT JELLY *pictured on page 19*

Here is another of Judith Wilson's recipes, which she finds a very useful alternative to jelly made with apples, as the mint supply can be a bit sparse by the apple season. It works best with under-ripe or just-ripe gooseberries. **Judith says that the recipe works equally well with cooking apples**. See page 18 for useful information on making jellies.

1.3 kg (3 lb) gooseberries,
  washed and dried but no need to top and tail
1 bunch of fresh mint
425 ml (15 fl oz) vinegar
granulated sugar (see step 4)
2 tablespoons finely chopped fresh mint

1 Put the gooseberries in a heavy-based pan with enough water to cover them. Add the bunch of mint and then bring to the boil and simmer until the gooseberries are soft – about 30 minutes.
2 Add the vinegar and cook for a further 5 minutes.
3 Remove from the heat, put the contents of the pan into a jelly bag and allow to drip into another container overnight.
4 Measure the liquid and put in a pan with sugar, allowing 450 g (1 lb) of sugar to each 575 ml (1 pint) of liquid.
5 Heat gently until the sugar has dissolved and then boil briskly until setting point is reached – about 15 minutes (see page 21). Remove any scum (see page 21).
6 Turn off the heat and cool slightly before stirring in the chopped mint.
7 Pot into small cooled, sterilised jars, cover and label (see pages 16 and 22).

NOTE ON HERBS IN JELLIES: Herb jellies are given extra appeal if you include either some of the chopped herb in the jelly or suspend a sprig in it. However, there can sometimes be a problem with the chopped herb or sprig rising in the jar. Terry Clarke seems to have solved this by using the prepared herb wet, but not soaking, and adding it after setting point is reached. Terry freezes finely chopped mint specifically for this purpose.

This recipe was e-mailed to me by Dylan Roys, of BBC Radio Lincolnshire. He has covered many a WI event and WI Market all around Lincolnshire and we receive excellent coverage of our activities in the Federation as well as having our own live 20-minute slot every two weeks throughout the year. This recipe came about following Dylan's trip out to see Bill, 'The Fulbeck Walnut Man'. Dylan says: 'I've always been a big fan of pickled walnuts although I must admit they are an acquired taste. Mother once had a huge sweet jar which lasted many years and they improved with age.

'Anyone looking for pickled walnuts in the shop will know how expensive they are, which is a pity because they are so easy to put down. The **shop-bought ones are also a pale imitation of the real home-pickled ones.** There are many recipes but on a recent trip out with my mate Bill, he gave me some good tips. Walnuts need to be picked in the green before the shell inside has formed. **Bill tells me Wimbledon week is a good bet.** Not every year will produce a good crop of walnuts so make enough to last through a bad season.'

I then received another recipe for pickled walnuts from Margaret Hanford, who tells me that her neighbour has a huge walnut tree in his garden and this year (2001) the tree is laden with nuts. He reckons the latest date for picking is the 12th July. Margaret very kindly sends quantities for the brine and a sweetened spiced vinegar but otherwise the method is exactly as Dylan outlines.

DYLAN'S PICKLED WALNUTS

MAKES: enough to fill two 1.3 kg (3 lb) jars
PREPARATION & COOKING TIME:
1 hour + 3 days brining

about 4.5 kg (10 lb) green walnuts

FOR THE BRINE:
450 g (1 lb) salt and 4.5 litres (8 pints) water, or 50 g (2 oz) salt per 575 ml (1 pint) water

FOR THE SWEETENED SPICED VINEGAR:
**1.7 litres (3 pints) malt vinegar
450 g (1 lb) brown sugar
1½ teaspoons salt
1 teaspoon pickling spice
1 teaspoon black peppercorns
½ teaspoon whole cloves**

1 To make the brine, stir the salt into the water until the salt has dissolved.
2 Once you have picked your walnuts, put on a pair of rubber gloves. This is vital because walnuts will produce a brown stain which give the fingers the appearance of those of a 40-a-day smoker! Take a fork and prick each walnut three or four times. Put them in a jar and cover them with the brine overnight. Repeat the process for three days, using fresh salt water each time.
3 Rinse the walnuts in clean water to remove excess salt. The walnuts should then be placed on a tray outside or in a window to dry until they blacken. This takes about a day.
4 To make the spiced vinegar, put all the ingredients in a pan and bring to the boil. Boil for 5–10 minutes. Once the walnuts are black, place them in a sterilised jar and cover with the sweetened spiced vinegar. Seal and label (see pages 16 and 22). They will take about 6 months to become mature enough.

NOTES: The walnuts can be covered with unsweetened spiced vinegar, if preferred.
It's an idea to make several smaller jars and fill with different aromatic flavourings. Chillies, peppers and sugar are all possible.

Orange Slices in Spiced Honey (page 60)

AUTUMN PRESERVES

ROWAN BERRY & APPLE JELLY

JANE'S MANGO CHUTNEY

MAKES: about 1.3 kg (3 lb)
PREPARATION TIME: 30 minutes
COOKING TIME: 20 minutes

This is one of Connie Stennett's (of Coningsby and Tattershall WI) grandma's recipes,from 1923. The apples in it can be replaced with quinces and Connie reckons a cinnamon stick added to the fruit is a nice variation. I've left it as Connie wrote it out for me, straight from the page of her grandma's book.

Take equal quantities of rowan berries and apples (or quinces). Put in preserving pan and cover well with water. Boil slowly until very soft. Strain through jelly bag. Then add 1 lb sugar to each pint of juice and boil for 20 minutes.
   It should be the colour of amber and quite clear.

ROWAN BERRY & ROSEMARY APPLE JELLY: Add some chopped fresh rosemary leaves to this or to plain apple jelly (which can be rather bland if no other flavour is added to it).
   Rosemary is available all year round but it is a woody herb, which makes it slightly chewy and it can sink to the bottom of the jar. Terry Clarke finds that chopping the rosemary leaves and then boiling for 5 minutes allows sufficient moisture to be absorbed to soften them and that makes rosemary suspend beautifully, too.

This recipe was sent to Connie Stennett by her daughter, Jane, from America. Serve with any curry, or tandoori dishes or cold cuts. It can be used immediately but will develop even more flavour on keeping.

1 tablespoon raisins
6 dried chillies, ground or crumbled
2.5 cm (1-inch) piece of fresh root ginger, shredded
1 teaspoon chilli powder
1 teaspoon black peppercorns, lightly crushed
115 ml (4 fl oz) vinegar
225 g (8 oz) sugar
3 teaspoons salt
2 garlic cloves, crushed
6 green mangoes, peeled and sliced, stones discarded

1 Soak the raisins in just enough water to cover them for 10–15 minutes.
2 Mix together the chillies, ginger, chilli powder and peppercorns.
3 Boil together the vinegar, sugar and salt. Add the chilli-paste mixture, with the garlic and 115 ml (4 fl oz) of water. Cook for 2 minutes.
4 Add the prepared mangoes and simmer for 10–12 minutes. Add the drained raisins .
5 Spoon into cooled, sterilised jars, seal and label (see pages 16 and 22).

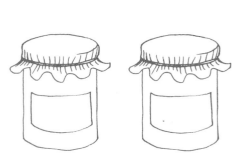

MAKES: about 900 g (2 lb)
PREPARATION TIME: 15 minutes + minimum 2 hours standing
COOKING TIME: 1 hour

SPICED APPLE JELLY
pictured on page 15

A delicious recipe from Terry Clarke, who recommends this to serve with roast pork or lamb as well as for delicious sandwiches.

900 g (2 lb) cooking apples, chopped, no need to peel or core
2 lemons, sliced
25 g (1 oz) fresh root ginger, chopped
1 cinnamon stick
1/2 teaspoon cloves
sugar (see step 3)

1 Place the apples and 1.7 litres (3 pints) of water in a preserving pan, with the lemons, ginger and spices. Bring to the boil and simmer for 45 minutes to an hour, or until the apples are very soft.
2 Pour into a jelly bag and leave to strain for at least 2 hours.
3 Measure the juice and add 450 g (1 lb) sugar for each 575 ml (1 pint) of juice.
4 Dissolve over a gentle heat and then bring to a boil until setting point is reached (see page 21). Remove any scum (see page 21).
5 Pour into cooled, sterilised jars and seal (see pages 16 and 22). Label and store.

MAKES: about 2.5 kg (5½ lb)
PREPARATION TIME: 30 minutes
COOKING TIME: about 1½ hours

PUMPKIN MARMALADE
pictured on page 45

This, with Pumpkin Chutney (page 57), is a recipe we used at Denman College when we had an enormous specimen presented to us. Pumpkin makes a lovely marmalade, with a beautiful colour.

1.5 kg (3 lb 5 oz) pumpkin, peeled, all seeds
   and fibre removed, and then flesh sliced
1 litre (1¾ pints) water
675 g (1½ lb) oranges, halved and sliced thinly
675 g (1½ lb) lemons, halved and sliced thinly
80 g (3 oz) fresh root ginger, shredded finely
1.3 kg (3 lb) granulated sugar

1 Place the pumpkin in a large pan, with the water, oranges, lemons and ginger. Bring to the boil and then simmer for 45 minutes– 1 hour until the citrus peel is very soft.
2 Add the sugar, stirring until it has dissolved. Return to the boil and then cook over a medium heat until the mixture is thick enough for a wooden spoon to be drawn through the centre to leave a clear channel.
3 Pour the marmalade into cooled, sterilised jars and seal with waxed discs or twist top lids (see pages 16 and 22). Label and store.

BRAMBLE & APPLE CURD *pictured opposite right*

MAKES: about 1.1–1.3 kg (2–3 lb)
PREPARATION TIME: 20 minutes
COOKING TIME: about 20 minutes in
microwave or 40 minutes in bowl over water

450 g (1 lb) brambles (blackberries)
450 g (1 lb) prepared weight peeled,
cored and chopped cooking apples
grated zest and juice of 2 lemons
450 g (1 lb) caster sugar
4 eggs, beaten
115 g (4 oz) butter, preferably unsalted

This is quick and easy to make, a gorgeous colour and delicious to eat. Use it in the same way as lemon curd, for fillings, folded through yoghurt or just spooned on to wholemeal toast or muffins – you don't need butter.

I like to cook fruit curds in the microwave and prefer them to have a smooth consistency. Therefore, I usually sieve the fruit pulp to remove the bramble seeds and again at the end, if necessary, to remove any cooked egg bits. If you prefer a chunkier result, simply mash the fruit down with a fork or potato masher.

1 Cook the fruit with lemon zest and 2 tablespoons of water in a pan (or in the microwave) until pulpy. Purée the fruit by passing it through a sieve.
2 Transfer to a bowl if necessary, add the lemon juice and sugar and stir until the sugar is dissolved. Beat the eggs and strain on to the fruit pulp.
3 Cook over a saucepan of water on a low heat or in the microwave, stirring occasionally, until a thick and creamy consistency is obtained. Strain the curd, to remove the bramble seeds and any bits of cooked egg.
4 Pour into cooled sterilised jars and cover with a waxed disc and cellophane cover (see pages 16 and 22). Label and store in the fridge for up to 6 weeks.

AUTUMN MARMALADE *pictured opposite centre*

MAKES: 4.5 kg (10 lb)
PREPARATION TIME: 1 hour
COOKING TIME: 2–2½ hours

450 g (1 lb) lemons, chopped roughly
after removing pips, pips reserved
450 g (1 lb) limes, as for lemons
1 litre (1¾ pints) water
675 g (1½ lb) cooking apples, peeled,
cored and chopped
2.7 kg (6 lb) sugar

This has a lovely flavour and the apples give the marmalade a more unusual texture. Make sure that you cook the citrus fruit well before adding the sugar and apples.

1 Place the lemons and limes in a large pan, with the water. Place the pips in a muslin bag and add to the pan. Bring to the boil and simmer for about 2 hours, until the fruit is soft and the contents of the pan are reduced in volume by about half.
2 Squeeze the bag of pips to extract the pectin and set aside. Liquidise the fruit, using some of the liquid, until it is completely smooth. Return the purée to the pan and stir into the remaining cooking liquid.
4 Meanwhile, cook the apples over a very low heat until soft – you could use the microwave for this. Add to the citrus mixture, with the sugar.
5 Stir until the sugar is dissolved and then bring to the boil. Boil rapidly until setting point is reached (see page 21). Remove any scum (see page 21).
6 Pour into cooled, sterilised jars and seal (see pages 16 and 22). Label and store.

From left to right: Pumpkin Marmalade (page 43); Autumn Marmalade (above); Bramble and Apple Curd (above)

MAKES: about 2.2–2.7 kg (5–6 lb)
PREPARATION TIME: about 40 minutes
COOKING TIME: about 2 hours

MAKES: about 2.2 kg (5 lb)
PREPARATION TIME: soaking apricots overnight + 20 minutes

BEETROOT & GINGER CHUTNEY

DIANA'S UNCOOKED CHUTNEY

This is one of the first chutneys I ever made and it remains one of my favourites. I suppose the earthy smell and flavour of the beetroot reminds me of my Dad's fruit and vegetable garden when, as a child, I used to help harvest everything. I have never had much success with gardening and I am happy to buy the products of other people's hard labour, either locally or from my WI Market.

1.3 kg (3 lb) beetroot, cooked
450 g (1 lb) onions, chopped
1.1 litres (2 pints) vinegar
450 g (1 lb) cooking apples, peeled and chopped
450 g (1 lb) seedless raisins or dates, chopped
3 tablespoons ground ginger
1 teaspoon salt
900 g (2 lb) granulated sugar

1 Peel and cut the beetroot into cubes or mash well if a smoother chutney is preferred.
2 Place the onion in a large preserving pan, with a little of the vinegar, and cook for a few minutes, to soften the onion. Add the apples, raisins or dates and continue cooking until pulpy.
3 Add the beetroot, ginger, salt and half the remaining vinegar. Simmer gently until thick.
4 Stir in the sugar and remaining vinegar and continue cooking until thick again.
5 Pot into cooled, sterilised jars, seal with a vinegar-proof lid and label (see pages 16 and 22). Store for 6–8 weeks before using.

I have always steered away from uncooked chutneys and relishes as we are not allowed to sell them in WI Markets because of possible fermentation. But those that I have tasted elsewhere have always been very good. This recipe was a popular choice for a Denman College swap-shop on the 'Preserves' course last year and was brought along by Diana Cuthbert of Surrey WI Federation. My step-mum, Eileen, makes a very similar one with dates and apple.

225 g (8 oz) dried apricots
900 g (2 lb) Bramley cooking apples
225 g (8 oz) sultanas
225 g (8 oz) dates, stoned
450 g (1 lb) onions
2 garlic cloves
350 g (12 oz) light soft brown sugar
425 ml (15 fl oz) malt vinegar
1 teaspoon ground ginger

1 Place the apricots in a bowl and cover with water. Leave to soak overnight and then drain (or see page 17). If you use 'no-need-to-soak' dried apricots, you can omit this step.
2 Mince all the fruits and onion and garlic together or finely chop in a food processor. Add the sugar, vinegar and ginger.
3 Stir well and spoon into cooled, sterilised jars, seal with vinegar-proof covers and label (see pages 16 and 22). Store in a cool, dark place for at least 3 months before using.

MAKES: 3.2–3.6 kg (7–8 lb)
PREPARATION TIME: 30 minutes
COOKING TIME: 1 hour

HIGH DUMPSY DEARIE JAM

I cannot resist passing on this recipe, even if just to preserve its delightful name! No one seems to know where the name comes from but it is thought to originate in Worcestershire. It was always a great conversation piece at the Royal Show at Stoneleigh in Warwickshire, where WI Markets had a selling stand in the WI Pavilion. The passage behind the selling area was affectionately known as 'the jam run' as the walls were lined with shelves bearing every imaginable variety of jam, jelly, marmalade, chutney and pickle! They were all in alphabetical order so that we could quickly find a particular variety for a discerning customer. Other stand-holders used to bring their boxes to stock up with jars for the storecupboard to keep them going through the year. The jam is a delicious variety to use in traditional puddings, such as jam roly-poly and steamed sponge.

900 g (2 lb) cooking apples, peeled, cored and sliced
900 g (2 lb) pears, peeled, cored and sliced
900 g (2 lb) plums, halved and stoned
50 g (2 oz) fresh root ginger, bruised and tied in a muslin bag
2 kg (4½ lb) sugar
zest and juice of 1 lemon

1 Place all the fruit and ginger in a large pan and add just enough water to cover the base of the pan. Simmer until the fruit is tender – about 45 minutes.
2 Remove from the heat and add the sugar, stirring until dissolved. Add the lemon zest and juice.
3 Bring to the boil and cook rapidly until the setting point of the jam is reached – test after 15 minutes (see page 21). Remove any scum (see page 21).
4 Pour into cooled, sterilised jars (see pages 16 and 22), discarding the ginger, and seal. Label and store.

MAKES: 1.1–1.3 kg (2¼–3 lb)
PREPARATION TIME: 20 minutes, if using ready-cooked beetroot
COOKING TIME: 1 hour

ORANGE & BEETROOT JAM *pictured on page 49*

This is a delicious combination that is a rather nice change from the usual. It is very good with cheese and cold meats or with hot roast meats. It also makes an excellent accompaniment to a vegetarian nut roast. If you can't find the fresh beetroot to cook yourself, use the vacuum-packed, ready-cooked variety – saves a job. I found the recipe in Market Rasen WI's recipe book, compiled to celebrate its Golden Jubilee back in 1973; it was contributed by Shirley Sanderson.

900 g (2 lb) cooked beetroot, skinned and cut into strips
2 teaspoons grated zest of orange
150 ml (¼ pint) orange juice
150 ml (¼ pint) lemon juice
½ teaspoon ground cinnamon
3 oranges, peeled and cut into segments,
    reserve peel and pith and any pips
900 g (2 lb) sugar

1 Place the beetroot, orange zest, juices and cinnamon in a large preserving pan with 300 ml (½ pint) of water. Place the reserved peel, pith and pips in a muslin bag and add to the pan.
2 Bring to the boil and then simmer for 30 minutes.
3 Remove the bag and squeeze the bag to extract all the juice. Add the sugar and stir until completely dissolved. Add the orange segments.
4 Boil rapidly until setting point is reached (see page 21). Remove any scum (see page 21). Leave to stand for 5–10 minutes and then pour into cooled, sterilised jars and seal and label (see pages 16 and 22).

PLUM, GRAPE & CARDAMOM JELLY *pictured opposite*

MAKES: about 675 g (1½ lb)
PREPARATION TIME:
10 minutes + minimum 2 hours standing
COOKING TIME: about 1 hour

1.8 kg (4 lb) plums, any variety, stoned
and chopped roughly
225 g (8 oz) white grapes
225 g (8 oz) purple grapes
1 tablespoon crushed cardamom pods
sugar (see step 2)

Another delicious jelly from Terry Clarke, which Terry recommends to serve with roast beef as well as in the usual way as a spread.

1 Place the fruit and cardamoms with 575 ml (1 pint) water in a preserving pan and bring slowly to the boil. Simmer until all the ingredients are cooked, mashing down the fruit to release all the flavours – about 30–45 minutes.
2 Pour into a jelly bag and leave to drip – a minimum of 2 hours. Measure the juice and take a pectin test (page 20), adding citric acid if necessary. To each 575 ml (1 pint) of juice, add 450 g (1 lb) granulated sugar.
3 Dissolve over a low heat. Bring to the boil and boil rapidly until setting point is reached (see page 21). Remove any scum (see page 21).
4 Pour into cooled, sterilised jars and seal (see pages 16 and 22). Label and store.

PLUM POT *pictured opposite*

MAKES: about four 450 g (1 lb) jars
PREPARATION TIME:
20 minutes + standing overnight
COOKING TIME: about 45 minutes

1.3 kg (3 lb) plums, washed, stoned and
chopped into large pieces
450 g (1 lb) raisins or sultanas
2 large oranges (175–225 g/6–8 oz each),
sliced and chopped into small pieces
1.3 kg (3 lb) sugar

Helen Snee, of Willingham-by Stow WI, submitted this recipe for our WI Federation's *Millennium Cookbook*. Helen says she got the original idea from a magazine years ago and this is the version she brings out every time she has a good plum crop. Helen uses sultanas with Victoria or greengage plums and raisins and a dark brown sugar with dark plums. The recipe has also been made using fresh apricots. I've seen a similar recipe which adds rum and crunchy flaked almonds – sounds delicious: Rum Plum Pot!

1 Put all the fruit and the sugar into a large non-metallic bowl. Cover and leave overnight.
2 Next day, transfer the mixture to a large preserving pan and heat slowly until the sugar is dissolved, stirring all the time.
3 Bring to the boil and then simmer until the mixture is fairly thick – about 30 minutes. A knob of butter can be added during cooking, to reduce any scum.
4 Pour into cooled, sterilised jars and seal (see pages 16 and 22). Label and store.

Clockwise from top left: Plum Pot (above); Plum, Grape & Cardamom Jelly (above); Red Tomato & Celery Chutney (page 50); Orange & Beetroot Jam (page 47)

MAKES: about 2.7 kg (6 lb)
PREPARATION TIME: 45 minutes
COOKING TIME: 2–2¹/₂ hours

RED TOMATO & CELERY CHUTNEY *pictured on page 49*

This is a lovely chutney found in the WI magazine *Home and Country* a few years back. It uses celery, which is not often to be found in chutneys but here it marries very well with the tomatoes, making it an ideal accompaniment to cheeses, especially a particularly good strong one called Lincolnshire Poacher – but I would say that, wouldn't I?

450 g (1 lb) onions, chopped finely or processed
1 large or 2 small heads of celery, trimmed
    and chopped finely or processed
900 ml (1¹/₂ pints) malt vinegar
50 g (2 oz) whole pickling spices, e.g., peppercorns, allspice berries,
    ginger, celery seeds and dried chillies, tied in muslin
1 kg (2¹/₄ lb) ripe tomatoes, skinned and chopped
450 g (1 lb) cooking apples, peeled, cored
    and finely chopped or processed
2 teaspoons salt
a good pinch of cayenne pepper
350 g (12 oz) light soft brown sugar
225 g (8 oz) sultanas or raisins, chopped roughly

1   Place the onions and celery, with half the vinegar and the bag of spices, in a large preserving pan. Bring to the boil and then simmer for about 30 minutes, until almost tender.
2   Add the tomatoes and apples, the remaining vinegar and the other ingredients. Bring slowly to the boil, stirring frequently, and continue to cook slowly, uncovered for 1¹/₂–2 hours, or until the chutney is thick and there is no liquid left on the surface. Stir from time to time, to prevent sticking.
3   Remove the muslin bag and then spoon the chutney into cooled, sterilised jars and seal with a vinegar-proof top (see pages 16 and 22). Label and store for 2–3 weeks before use.

MAKES: about 2.7 kg (6 lb)
PREPARATION TIME: 30 minutes + standing overnight
COOKING TIME: about 2 hours

AUNT MARY'S GREEN TOMATO CHUTNEY

There must be so many green tomatoes around come autumn because there seems to be a never-ending supply of recipes for green tomato chutney. This one is from Betty Grant, who worked with me on Market Rasen WI Market for several years and was very popular for her croissants and cream horns. She remembers having this at her Aunt Mary's when she was at college.

Amazingly, most of the chutneys I've come across are basically the same, using similar quantities of tomatoes, apples and onions. The variations come with the type of dried fruit used, the spices and different sugars, from plain granulated through to the light and dark soft browns and muscovados – the choice is yours. Betty uses sultanas but you could use raisins or dates.

1.3 kg (3 lb) green tomatoes
675 g (1¹/₂ lb) cooking apples
675 g (1¹/₂ lb) onions
2 tablespoons salt
350 g (12 oz) sugar
2 teaspoons ground mixed spice
225 g (8 oz) sultanas
575 ml (1 pint) malt vinegar

1   Mince the tomatoes, apples and onions. Place in a large bowl and sprinkle over the salt. Cover and leave overnight.
2   Next day, pour off the liquid that has been drawn out by the salt and discard it. Transfer everything to a large preserving pan. Bring to the boil, with the vinegar, and then add the sugar, spice and fruit.
3   Bring to the boil and then simmer until soft and pulpy, about 1¹/₂ hours.
4   Spoon into cooled, sterilised jars, seal with a vinegar-proof lid and label (see pages 16 and 22). Store for 6–8 weeks, to mature, before using.

MAKES: enough to fill a 425 ml (15 fl oz) jar
PREPARATION TIME: 10 minutes
COOKING TIME: 10 minutes

CINNAMON GRAPE PICKLE *pictured on page 15*

This is an unusual and quite delicious pickle from Terry Clarke, which is particularly good with smoked meats and with pork loin, duck and chicken. Terry says that the balsamic vinegar and the cinnamon give the pickle a warm mellowness but that it is the 'little zippy splat' each time you bite into a grape that makes it really addictive. Terry also serves these along with the olives and other nibbles with drinks.

275 g (10 oz) white sugar
225 ml (8 fl oz) white-wine vinegar
1 tablespoon balsamic vinegar
1/2 tablespoon cracked peppercorns
1 cinnamon stick
350 g (12 oz) white or black seedless grapes

1   Put the sugar and vinegars into a small saucepan and stir over a low heat until the sugar is dissolved. Raise the heat and add the peppercorns and cinnamon stick and boil for 5–6 minutes.
2   While the syrup is boiling, de-stalk enough grapes to fill your chosen jar. Remove and wash them under cold water, drain thoroughly and dry with kitchen paper. Return to the cooled, sterilised jar (see page 16), ensuring that they are firmly positioned but being careful not to bruise the fruit.
3   Remove the cinnamon stick from the pan and insert it in the jar. Pour over the boiling syrup, filling right to the top. Cover tightly with a vinegar-proof lid (see page 22) and store in a cool place for 3–4 weeks before use. It will keep for up to a year. If using white grapes, remember to store them out of the light to prevent them from discolouring.

MAKES: about three 450 g (1 lb) jars
PREPARATION TIME: 20 minutes
COOKING TIME: 25 minutes

SPICED PEARS IN RASPBERRY VINEGAR

Try this lovely recipe using your Raspberry Vinegar (page 38) – the unsweetened version – or you can use a bought raspberry or red-wine vinegar. The pears are delicious served as an unusual accompaniment to cold turkey or a game pie at Christmas. This recipe was given to a group of WI members from the East Midlands area at Brackenhurst College in Nottinghamshire, by Susan Jervis of Shropshire. The weekend course followed a week's work at the Royal Show in Warwickshire, from whence Terry Clarke and I managed to procure the most fantastic range of soft fruits imaginable from one of the major supermarket displays there, which would otherwise have been destroyed. We had great fun making as many preserves as possible with as many different combinations as we could think of.

900 g (2 lb) firm eating pears, peeled, cored and quartered
450 g (1 lb) granulated sugar
450 ml (16 fl oz) raspberry vinegar
1 cinnamon stick
1 teaspoon whole cloves
1 teaspoon allspice berries

1   Place the pears in a pan and cover with boiling water. Simmer for 5 minutes.
2   Drain in a colander, saving 300 ml (1/2 pint) of the cooking water.
3   Mix the sugar, the reserved water and the vinegar in the pan. Heat and stir until the sugar dissolves. Add the spices and pears and simmer gently until the pears are translucent – about 20 minutes.
4   Drain the pears, reserving the cooking liquid, and place in cooled, sterilised jars (see page 16). Remove any scum from the liquid. Pour the liquid, including the spices, over the pears to cover. Cover with vinegar-proof lids, label and store (see page 22).

MAKES: about 2.2 kg (5 lb)
PREPARATION TIME: about 30 minutes
COOKING TIME: about 2 hours

ORCHARD JAM

I found this recipe in an old magazine when I was preparing for my 'Harvest Home' course at Denman College a couple of years ago. It's a sort of cross between jam and marmalade in texture and flavour and, like all home-made jam, makes a delicious topping for a steamed sponge pudding. The combined weight of the fruits needs to be around 1.3 kg (3 lb) but don't worry if the proportion of each fruit varies slightly.

225 g (8 oz) oranges, juice squeezed, pips and peel reserved
225 g (8 oz) grapefruits, juice squeezed, pips and peel reserved
225 g (8 oz) lemons, juice squeezed, pips and peel reserved
350 g (12 oz) large cooking apples, peeled, cored and quartered,
core reserved
350 g (12 oz) large pears, peeled, cored and quartered, core reserved
1.7 litres (3 pints) water
1.3 kg (3 lb) granulated sugar

1 Cut the citrus peel into thin strips. Tie the apple and pear cores and the citrus pips in a piece of muslin.
2 Put the fruit, juice, peel and muslin bag into a large saucepan, with the water.
3 Simmer gently for 2 hours or until the fruit is very soft and the mixture is reduced by almost half.
4 Press the contents of the bag through a sieve and return the resulting thick purée to the pan. Add the sugar and stir until dissolved.
5 Bring to the boil and boil vigorously for 15 minutes or until setting point is reached (see page 20). Remove any scum (see page 20).
6 Pour into cooled, sterilised jars, seal and label (see pages 16 and 22).

MAKES: about 2.2 kg (5 lb)
PREPARATION TIME: about 1 hour
COOKING TIME: about 1½ hours

HEDGEROW JAM

My friend, Thea Hogg, is Musical Director of the Choral Society with which I sing and for which I am secretary — about the only thing I do which is not WI-connected. Thea often brings eggs and garden produce to choir rehearsals from her large garden set on the edge of the Lincolnshire Wolds. She has fantastic views over my part of the world over to Lincoln Cathedral and across to the Trent Valley and the Humber Bridge. Thea gave me this recipe, which she discovered when living near Kingston-upon-Thames in Surrey — not exactly a rural area, but Thea says the ingredients were easy to find.

225 g (8 oz) rose hips
225 g (8 oz) haws
225 g (8 oz) rowan berries
225 g (8 oz) sloes
450 g (1 lb) crab apples
450 g (1 lb) blackberries
450 g (1 lb) elderberries
115 g (4 oz) hazelnuts, chopped
900 g (2 lb) sugar plus equivalent to weight of fruit pulp (see step 3)

1 Wash and clean all the fruit well. Put the rose hips, haws, rowan berries, sloes and crab apples in a large preserving pan and add water to cover. Cook until all the fruit is tender — about 1 hour.
2 Sieve the fruits and weigh the resulting pulp. Put the pulp back into the washed preserving pan and add the blackberries, elderberries and chopped nuts. Simmer for about 15 minutes.
3 Add the 900 g (2 lb) of sugar plus as much extra sugar as the weight of the pulp. Cook over a low heat to dissolve the sugar and then boil rapidly until setting point is reached (see page 21). Remove any scum (see page 21).
4 Pour into cooled, sterilised jars, seal and label (see pages 16 and 22).

MAKES: about 675–900 g (1 1/2–2 lb)
PREPARATION TIME: 30 minutes
COOKING TIME: about 30 minutes

MAKES: six 450 g (1 lb) jars
PREPARATION TIME: 45 minutes
COOKING TIME: 20 minutes

WEST COUNTRY CURD

MANGO PICKLE

Yet another way of capturing the last of the sunshine and a delicious alternative to the more traditional lemon curd. This can also be cooked in a double saucepan or in a bowl over a pan of simmering water – I just prefer to use the microwave.

350 g (12 oz) cooking apples, cored and sliced, no need to peel
350 g (12 oz) pears, cored and sliced, no need to peel
grated zest and juice of 1 lemon
150 ml (1/4 pint) cider
350 g (12 oz) granulated sugar
115 g (4 oz) butter, preferably unsalted
4 eggs, beaten

1 Place the fruit and cider in a large bowl and cover with pierced cling film. Microwave on full power for 10–15 minutes or until the fruit is soft and pulpy.

2 Rub the fruit through a sieve and return to the bowl. Add the sugar and butter. Microwave on full power for 2 minutes and then stir well, making sure that the butter is melted and the sugar is dissolved.

3 Add the eggs and stir thoroughly. Continue cooking in the microwave until thick and the mixture coats the back of a spoon. Stir frequently. This can be done on full power or reduce the cooking power to medium and cook for a longer time.

4 Strain again into a jug. Pour the curd into cooled, sterilised jars, seal with a waxed disc and cover with cellophane (see pages 16 and 22). Store in the fridge for up to 6 weeks. Once opened, eat within 2 weeks.

This pickle is rather a change from the usual mango chutney. It was sent to me by Margaret Hanford, of Quorn, in Leicestershire, who has written many books herself. Margaret says it is an excellent way to preserve mangoes; look out for boxes of mangoes which can be bought on markets up and down the country.

3.6 kg (8 lb) ripe mangoes, peeled
pared zest of 1/2 lemon
15 g (1/2 oz) whole cloves
15 g (1/2 oz) whole allspice berries
7 g (1/4 oz) fresh root ginger
7 g (1/4 oz) cinnamon sticks
1.1 litres (2 pints) distilled or malt vinegar
1.8 kg (4 lb) sugar

1 Cut slices of flesh from the mangoes down to the stone, so that each mango provides 10–12 slices.

2 Place the lemon zest and spices in a muslin bag and secure. Place the vinegar and sugar in a large pan and heat slowly, stirring continuously, until the sugar is dissolved.

3 Add the fruit and the bag of spices and simmer until the fruit is tender but not too soft.

4 Remove the bag of spices and drain the fruit. Pack into cooled, sterilised jars (see page 16). Pour the syrup back into the pan and bring to the boil.

5 Boil the syrup until it starts to thicken and then pour over the fruit. Seal with vinegar-proof tops (see page 22). Keep any leftover vinegar syrup and use to top up the jars if necessary, as the fruit absorbs the liquid on standing. Allow to mature for at least a month before use.

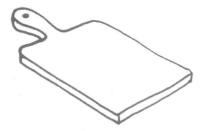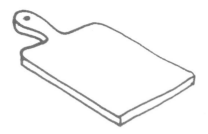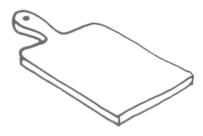

This is a variation suggested in the recipe which appeared in *A Taste of WI Markets*, a cookbook which I helped to edit for the Markets' 75th Anniversary in 1994. I first used the variation at Denman College on a '**Preserves**' course, when we were inundated with marrow. In the reverse situation – a glut of apples instead of marrow – just double the amount of apple.

MAKES: about 2.2 kg (5 lb)
PREPARATION TIME: about 30 minutes +
overnight or several hours soaking
COOKING TIME: about 1½ hours

450 g (1 lb) dried apricots, chopped
450 g (1 lb) prepared marrow, diced
**450 g (1 lb) cooking apples, peeled
and quartered**
350 g (12 oz) onions, chopped
**2 teaspoons each whole cloves,
cardamom seeds and peppercorns**
80 g (3 oz) fresh root ginger, bruised
575 ml (1 pint) white malt vinegar
450 g (1 lb) granulated sugar

This chutney is particularly good in a cheese sandwich but goes equally well with cold meats or as an alternative to apple sauce as an accompaniment for roast pork .

1 Cover the apricots with water and soak for several hours or overnight. (See page 17 for a microwave shortcut.) If you have 'no-need-to-soak' apricots, you can omit this step.
2 Pour into a large preserving pan. Add the marrow, apple and onion. Tie the whole spices and ginger in a piece of muslin and add to the mixture. Cook until the apples are pulpy, adding more water if necessary to prevent sticking; stir occasionally. This will take about 20 minutes.
3 Add the vinegar and sugar and simmer, uncovered, until all the liquid has been absorbed.
4 Pot into cooled sterilised jars, seal with a vinegar-proof lid and label (see pages 16 and 22). Store for 6–8 weeks before using.

APRICOT, MARROW & WALNUT CHUTNEY: Add 115 g (4 oz) of chopped walnuts towards the end of the cooking time.

APRICOT & MARROW CHUTNEY

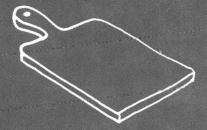 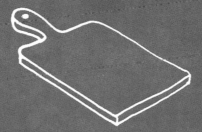 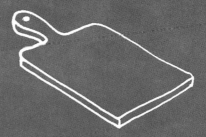

I think this recipe struck a chord with me when I spotted it in the WI magazine *Home and Country* a few years back, as my husband, Roy, and I started married life together in 'Orchard Cottage'. It certainly brings together **the traditional autumn fruits and vegetables** and **conjures up a country feel** with its title.

MAKES: 2.7 kg (6 lb)
PREPARATION TIME: about 45 minutes
COOKING TIME: about 2 hours

900 g (2 lb) plums, washed, halved and stoned
900 g (2 lb) ripe tomatoes, skinned and sliced
850 ml (1½ pints) malt vinegar
6 garlic cloves
450 g (1 lb) onions
225 g (8 oz) raisins
1.1 kg (2¼ lb) cooking apples, peeled and cored
450 g (1 lb) demerara sugar
25 g (1 oz) salt
50 g (2 oz) whole pickling spices, e.g. peppercorns, allspice berries, ginger, celery seeds and dried chillies, tied in a muslin bag

Even if you haven't got a garden in which to grow and harvest, friends, family or someone in the neighbourhood may be happy to off-load the odd pound or two of produce, especially if there is a glut or a particularly good crop. If not, visit one of the growing number of farm shops or pick-your-own places or call in to your nearest WI, Farmers' or local market for some of the best and freshest produce around. There are also lots of roadside/outside the garden gate stalls around at this time of year, offering really excellent produce at unbeatable prices.

1   Put the plums, tomatoes and vinegar into a large preserving pan. Bring to the boil and then simmer gently until very soft.
2   Mince together the garlic, onions, raisins and apples, or use a food processor to chop them finely. Add to the plum mixture, with the sugar, salt and bag of spices.
3   Heat gently until the sugar is dissolved. Bring to the boil and then simmer uncovered for about 2 hours, or until the chutney is well reduced and very thick. Stir from time to time, to prevent sticking.
4   Spoon into cooled, sterilised jars and seal with a vinegar-proof lid (see pages 16 and 22). Label and store for 2–3 weeks before use.

ORCHARD COTTAGE CHUTNEY

MAKES: 2.7 kg (6 lb)
PREPARATION TIME: 20 minutes
COOKING TIME: 30 minutes

PLUM & MULLED WINE JAM

This recipe was devised by former WI Country Markets Director, Judi Binns, once of Hertfordshire and now living in Yorkshire.

1.8 kg (4 lb) red plums, halved and stoned
**$1/2$ bottle of red wine
(whatever is cheap or on offer)**
mulled wine spices, e.g., cinnamon, nutmeg, cloves or your own choice
piece of orange zest without pith
1.8 kg (4 lb) sugar

1 Put the plums and wine into a preserving pan.
2 Place the spices and zest in a spice ball or muslin bag and add to the pan. Cook gently for 15–20 minutes or until the skins are soft.
3 Remove the spice ball or bag and add the sugar, stirring until dissolved. Bring to the boil and boil rapidly for about 10 minutes or until setting point is reached (see page 21). Remove any scum (see page 21).
4 Pot into cooled, sterilised jars, seal and label (see pages 16 and 22).

MAKES: about six 450 g (1 lb) jars
PREPARATION & COOKING TIME: about 1 hour

CUMBERLAND BEAN PICKLE

There are several versions of this available and sometimes it is, mistakenly, called a chutney. It uses similar ingredients to piccalilli, in which the raw vegetables are brined and then cooked and mixed in a hot spiced sauce. In this pickle, however, the vegetables are simply cooked in lightly salted water before being mixed with the sauce. This was given by Kathryn Wall of the Clwyd–Flint WI Federation.

900 g (2 lb) prepared weight trimmed and thinly sliced runner beans
450 g (1 lb) onions, sliced finely
a pinch of salt
425 ml (15 fl oz) white malt vinegar
50 g (2 oz) plain flour (some recipes use cornflour)
1 tablespoon mustard powder
$1/2$ teaspoon ground black pepper
$1/2$ teaspoon ground turmeric
150 g (5 oz) white sugar

1 Put the beans and onions in a pan with a pinch of salt and just enough water to cover. Bring to the boil and then simmer until tender – about 20 minutes.
2 In another large pan, mix together a tablespoon of vinegar, the flour and the spices to a smooth paste. Start to heat gently, adding the rest of the vinegar very carefully bit by bit, as you would for a roux sauce, ensuring that there are no lumps.
3 Simmer gently for 2–3 minutes, until the flour is cooked.
4 Add the sugar and stir well to make sure it is dissolved. Bring the sauce to the boil. It should be thick and shiny.
5 Drain the beans and onions and add to the sauce. Stir well and bring the mixture back to the boil. Continue cooking for about 10 minutes.
6 Spoon the mixture into cooled, sterilised jars and seal with a vinegar-proof cover (see pages 16 and 22). Label and store.

CARROT & RUNNER BEAN PICKLE: Add 450 g (1 lb) of peeled and sliced carrots and cook along with the beans and onions.
Add more sugar if you prefer a sweeter pickle. Also works well with broad beans and french beans.

MAKES: about 2.7 kg (6 lb)
PREPARATION TIME: about 30 minutes
COOKING TIME: 2–2¹/₂ hours

PUMPKIN CHUTNEY

This recipe is from an old WI *Home and Country* magazine. The 'Autumn Preserves' course students of the year 2000 were presented with a huge pumpkin: we made this chutney and Pumpkin Marmalade (page 43) and each student still had a big wedge each to take home!

Pumpkin makes a beautiful chutney, and, as with any chutney, the contents can be varied to suit your taste. The texture can be varied by cutting the fruits into larger pieces and, if you want a hotter chutney, add 3–4 fresh red chillies and 2–3 tablespoons of mustard seed.

675 g (1¹/₂ lb) prepared pumpkin, peeled, de-seeded and cut into 2.5 cm (1-inch) chunks
450 g (1 lb) cooking apples, peeled, cored and chopped coarsely
350 g (12 oz) onions, chopped
175 g (6 oz) sultanas or raisins
2 tablespoons salt
2 teaspoons ground ginger or 50 g (2 oz) fresh root ginger, shredded finely
¹/₂ teaspoon ground black pepper
2 teaspoons ground allspice
4–6 garlic cloves, crushed
575 ml (1 pint) malt or cider vinegar
450 g (1 lb) granulated or soft brown sugar
50 g (2 oz) stem ginger preserved in syrup, chopped finely (optional)

1 Put all ingredients, except the sugar and stem ginger, in a large preserving pan and mix well.
2 Bring to the boil and then reduce the heat and simmer for about 45 minutes, stirring occasionally, until the contents are very soft.
3 Stir in the sugar until dissolved and then continue to simmer, uncovered, for about 1–1¹/₂ hours or until the chutney is very thick and there is no liquid left on the surface.
4 Add the stem ginger, if using. Spoon into cooled, sterilised jars and seal with a vinegar-proof lid (see pages 16 and 22). Label and store for 6–8 weeks before use.

NOTE: Some cooks prefer to tie whole spices into a muslin bag, which is removed before potting the chutney; others prefer to use the ground spices, although this tends to give a cloudier result.

MAKES: about 1.8 kg (4 lb)
PREPARATION TIME: about 30 minutes
COOKING TIME: about 1 hour

SPICED PLUM CHUTNEY

Another recipe from Gill Worrell, for which you can use any type of plum. Gill says red plums produce a lovely colour and it is delicious served with smoked mackerel. It is cheap to produce when plums and apples are in plentiful supply. The cooking time can be reduced by cooking the plums, apples and onions in the microwave first.

675 g (1¹/₂ lb) plums, stoned and quartered
450 g (1 lb) onions, chopped
225 g (8 oz) cooking apples, peeled, cored and chopped
300 ml (¹/₂ pint) pickling malt vinegar
115 g (4 oz) sultanas
175 g (6 oz) soft brown sugar
1 cinnamon stick

1 Place all the ingredients in a large preserving pan. Bring to the boil and simmer, uncovered, for about 45 minutes, or until the chutney is thick and pulpy.
2 Spoon into cooled, sterilised jars and seal with a vinegar-proof cover (see pages 16 and 22). Label and store for at least 4–6 weeks before use.

PICCALILLI *pictured opposite, front*

MAKES: about 2.7 kg (6 lb)
PREPARATION TIME: about 45 minutes
COOKING TIME: 30 minutes

1 large cauliflower, broken into florets
450 g (1 lb) pickling onions, chopped
1.4 litres (2½ pints) white malt vinegar
900 g (2 lb) mixed vegetables,
diced or cut into 2.5 cm (1-inch) lengths;
choose from: french or runner beans,
cucumber, marrow or green tomatoes
2 fat cloves of garlic, crushed
450 g (1 lb) caster sugar
50 g (2 oz) dry mustard
115 g (4 oz) plain flour, sieved
25 g (1 oz) ground turmeric
1 teaspoon ground coriander
2 teaspoons salt

This is Terry Clarke's recipe, which, she admits, seems to break all the rules about brining vegetables, which is the usual procedure for this type of pickle. Terry says it works beautifully, produces a lovely piccalilli and keeps well if you can persuade the family to leave it for at least two weeks. Terry has kept it for up to nine months when, if anything, the flavour has improved!

1   In a large preserving pan, simmer the cauliflower and onions in 1.1 litres (2 pints) of the vinegar for 10 minutes.
2   Add the other vegetables, garlic and sugar and cook for a further 10 minutes.
3   Mix the mustard, flour, spices and salt with the remaining vinegar and add to the cooked vegetables, stirring all the time to prevent lumps from forming.
4   Stir well and simmer for a further 10 minutes.
5   Spoon into cooled, sterilised jars and cover with a vinegar-proof top (see pages 16 and 22). Label and store for 2 weeks before using.

MOSTARDA DI FRUTTA *pictured opposite, behind*

MAKES: about three 350 g (12 oz) jars
PREPARATION TIME:
15 minutes + 1 hour standing
COOKING TIME: about 15–20 minutes

115 g (4 oz) English mustard powder
115 g (4 oz) light soft brown sugar
300 ml (½ pint) white-wine vinegar
115 g (4 oz) each dried apricots, figs, raisins
and glacé cherries, chopped coarsely
50 g (2 oz) dried apple rings, chopped
6 pieces of stem ginger preserved in syrup,
chopped or sliced
1 teaspoon sea salt

Terry Clarke describes this as a tongue-tingling combination of **sweet and hot** rather than sweet and sour; it makes a classic accompaniment to ham and poultry, particularly at Christmas time.

1   In a bowl, put 300 ml (½ pint) of water and stir in the mustard. Cover and leave for at least 1 hour.
2   Place the sugar and vinegar in a saucepan and heat gently, stirring until the sugar is dissolved. Raise the heat and boil until the mixture starts to thicken.
3   Stir in the fruits, ginger, mustard and salt and return to the boil, stirring. Simmer until the mixture thickens.
4   Spoon into small jars or bottles, ensuring that there are no air bubbles, and seal with a vinegar-proof cover (see pages 16 and 22) Label and store in a cool, dark and dry place for 6–8 weeks before use.

MAKES: about four 450 g (1 lb) jars
PREPARATION TIME: 30 minutes
COOKING TIME: 1 hour 20 minutes

These make a lovely gift at Christmas time and look particularly attractive when presented with two or three other jars of different preserves. I've been using the recipe since starting the WI Market courses and it is always popular with the students.

6 oranges, cut into 5 mm (¼-inch) thick slices
450 ml (15 fl oz) white-wine or cider vinegar
350 g (12 oz) granulated sugar
115 g (4 oz) clear honey
1 teaspoon whole cloves
5 cm (2-inch) cinnamon stick
1 tablespoon coriander seeds, crushed
whole cloves, for decoration

ORANGE SLICES IN SPICED HONEY *pictured on page 41*

1 Place the orange slices in a pan with enough water to cover. Simmer for 45 minutes until the peel of the fruit is tender. Drain and discard the cooking water.
2 Put the vinegar, sugar, honey and spices into a pan and bring to the boil. Reduce to simmering point and then add the orange slices. Simmer gently for 15–20 minutes, until the zest of the fruit becomes translucent.
3 Strain off and reserve the vinegar and carefully pack the slices into cooled, sterilised jars. Placing two or three slices around the inside of the jar and then packing the remaining slices down the centre makes an attractive presentation.
4 If necessary, return the vinegar to the pan and boil rapidly for 5–10 minutes to reduce to a syrup.
5 Pour the syrup over the oranges, filling to the brim and removing any air bubbles by inserting a knife or wooden skewer to release the bubbles. Place one or two cloves in each jar as is is filled. Seal with vinegar-proof tops and label (see pages 16 and 22).

MAKES 1.3 kg (3 lb)
PREPARATION TIME: about 45 minutes + straining overnight
COOKING TIME: about 45 minutes

This jelly recipe comes from Christine Sherriff, who lives on a lovely farm near to Horncastle and is a member of Revesby and District WI. She and husband, Robert, converted derelict farm buildings into a purpose-built kitchen and teaching block a few years back. Christine teaches cookery there, including preserves, and I have done demonstrations and a cookery course there, which were most enjoyable times. Christine is now involved with Woodhall Spa WI Market and is the present Lincolnshire North WI Market Society Chairman.

1.8 kg (4 lb) blackberries
450 g (1 lb) sloes, washed and pricked with a needle
sugar (see step 2)

BLACKBERRY & SLOE JELLY

1 Put the blackberries and sloes into a preserving pan and cover with water. Bring to the boil and then lower the heat and simmer until the sloes are tender – about 20 minutes but this may vary according to which end of the season the sloes were picked.
2 Strain through a jelly bag, preferably overnight, and measure the juice. Allow 450 g (1 lb) of sugar to each 575 ml (1 pint) of juice.
3 Place the juice and sugar in the clean pan and heat gently, stirring until the sugar is dissolved. Boil hard to setting point (see page 21). Remove any scum (see page 21).
4 Pour into cooled, sterilised jars, seal and label (see pages 16 and 22).

From the back: Apricot & Orange Marmalade (page 62); Exotic Fruits Jam (page 62); Cranberry Curd (page 62)

WINTER PRESERVES

MAKES: about 2.7 kg (6 lb)
PREPARATION TIME: 30 minutes
COOKING TIME: about 2½ hours

This is easily my favourite marmalade and used to be that of my bed-and-breakfast guests, once they'd been persuaded to try something other than – plain seville orange.

450 g (1 lb) dried apricots
(use the no-need-to-soak ones), sliced,
chopped or scissor-snipped
675 g (1½ lb) seville oranges, washed, halved,
squeezed of juice and sliced thinly,
pips reserved
2 litres (3½ pints) water
2.2 kg (5 lb) sugar

APRICOT & ORANGE

MARMALADE *pictured on page 61*

1 Put the prepared fruit and the water in a large pan. Tie the pips and any membrane in a muslin bag and add to the pan. Bring to the boil and then simmer until the fruit is very soft and the contents are reduced by about half – about 2 hours.
2 Remove the muslin bag and squeeze the bag to extract all the juice. Add the sugar and stir until dissolved. Bring to a rolling boil and boil until setting point is reached – about 15–20 minutes (see page 21). Remove any scum (see page 21).
3 Pour into cooled, sterilised jars and seal (see pages 16 and 22). Label and store.

NOTE: If using ordinary dried apricots, add an extra 300 ml (½ pint) of water and leave to stand for at least 6 hours, or overnight.

MAKES: about 900 g (2 lb)
PREPARATION TIME: 10 minutes
COOKING TIME: 30–40 minutes

This makes a curd with a fabulous colour and would look great on the Christmas breakfast table or in a pretty pot for someone's Christmas present. A selection of Christmas preserves is even better and can be presented in an attractive basket or container for later use.

450 g (1 lb) cranberries
115 g (4 oz) unsalted butter
450 g (1 lb) caster sugar
4 large eggs, beaten and sieved

CRANBERRY

CURD *pictured on page 61*

1 Put the cranberries and 150 ml (¼ pint) of water in a saucepan and cook on a low heat until tender and popped – or you could cook them in the microwave.
2 Process them or pass through a sieve, if you prefer a smoother curd. Put back in the saucepan, with the butter and sugar, and heat until the butter is melted and the sugar is dissolved.
3 Add the eggs and stir the curd continuously over a low heat until thickened. If you are nervous of this, use a bowl over a pan of simmering water or the microwave. (See, for example, Lemon Curd, page 24.)
4 Pour into small cooled, sterilised jars and cover with a waxed disc and a cellophane cover (see pages 16 and 22). Store in the fridge for up to 6 weeks. Once opened, eat within 2 weeks.

MAKES: 1.3–1.8 kg (3–4 lb)
PREPARATION TIME: 20 minutes
COOKING TIME: 30–40 minutes

A real taste of summer sunshine to brighten winter days! This lovely combination needs no pre-cooking before adding the sugar.

900 g (2 lb) ripe pineapples,
skin and core removed,
cut into 1 cm (½-inch) pieces
450 g (1 lb) mangoes, peeled
and flesh cut into 1 cm (½-inch) pieces
grated zest and juice of 1 lemon, pips and
pith reserved and tied in a muslin bag
1.3 kg (3 lb) sugar

EXOTIC FRUITS

JAM *pictured on page 61*

1 Place the fruit and its juices, lemon zest and 4 tablespoons of juice (any remaining juice won't be needed), the muslin bag and the sugar in a large preserving pan. Heat gently and stir until all the sugar is dissolved.
2 Bring to the boil, and then reduce the heat and simmer for 30–40 minutes, or until setting point is reached (see page 21). Remove any scum (see page 21).
3 Pot into cooled, sterilised jars and seal (see pages 16 and 22). Label and store.

MAKES: about 4.5 kg (10 lb)
PREPARATION TIME: 1–1½ hours
COOKING TIME: 2½ hours

1.3 kg (3 lb) seville oranges
2 lemons
2.8 litres (5 pints) water
2.7 kg (6 lb) sugar

1 Wash and scrub the oranges and lemons. Cut the fruit in half and squeeze out the juice. Remove the pips and membrane and tie in a muslin bag.

2 Cut the peel into thin shreds (or coarse ones if preferred) and then place in a large preserving pan, with the juice, and the bag of pips and the water.

3 Bring to the boil and then simmer gently, uncovered, for about 2 hours, until the contents of the pan are reduced by about a half and the peel is really soft and tender.

4 Remove the muslin bag and squeeze the bag hard and carefully, to remove all the gooey liquid; this contains the pectin which is so important for a good set.

5 Add the sugar and stir until completely dissolved. Bring to the boil and boil rapidly until setting point is reached (see page 21).

6 Remove any scum from the surface (see page 21). Cool for 5–10 minutes.

7 Stir well to distribute the peel. Pour into cooled, sterilised jars and seal (see pages 16 and 22). Label and store.

TRADITIONAL SEVILLE ORANGE MARMALADE

This is the time-honoured traditional way of making marmalade with seville oranges. January into February is the time to make it, as this is the very short season for fresh sevilles, which are bitter oranges with a rough skin and a deep colour. The recipe is followed by several variations.

The preparation time will vary according to how you choose to prepare the peel but traditionalists will say that, if the peel is minced or processed, it is not, strictly speaking, marmalade! It is essential to allow enough cooking time for the peel to be really soft before adding the sugar, otherwise you will have a very tough and chewy marmalade.

CORIANDER MARMALADE: Add 1 tablespoon of crushed coriander seeds to the peel or pop them into the muslin bag when cooking, to enhance the orange flavour.

BLACK TREACLE MARMALADE: Add 2 tablespoons or more of black treacle with the sugar, for a different flavour and a rich colour.

BOOZY MARMALADE: Stir in 2–4 tablespoons of whisky or other spirit or liqueur per 2.7 kg (6 lb) quantity just before potting. To achieve a variety of boozy flavours from one batch, put 10 ml (2 teaspoons) of a different spirit or liqueur in each jar before pouring in the hot marmalade.

NUTTY MARMALADE: Add a few lightly toasted flaked almonds or chopped walnuts to your favourite recipe. Stir them in just before potting into jars.

EXTRA-FRUITY MARMALADE: For an extra fruity flavour, add a couple of peeled, cored and chopped cooking apples about 10 minutes before the end of the simmering time, when cooking the fruit peel.

GINGER MARMALADE: Add 115 g (4 oz) of finely chopped, crystallised ginger, or stem ginger preserved in syrup, at the same time as the sugar.

MAKES: about 4.5 kg (10 lb)
PREPARATION TIME: about 1 hour
COOKING TIME: about 2 hours

This is a delicious recipe I picked up from Sara Getley at Denman College, when we were working together on a WI Markets course.

MAKES: 5–5.4 kg (11–12 lb)
PREPARATION TIME: 5 minutes + about 30 minutes after initial cooking
COOKING TIME: 2–3 hours

I have been using this recipe for making marmalade for the last 10 or 11 years, since my sister, Rhoda, gave me one of Claire Macdonald's cookbooks for Christmas when she was living on the Isle of Skye. I love Claire's style of writing and I particularly like this method, although Claire tells me she cannot remember when she started doing it this way. I find it preferable to using a muslin bag to extract the pectin from the pith and pips. This is Claire's recipe from her book *Seasonal Cooking*.

RUM & RAISIN MARMALADE

675 g (1½ lb) sweet oranges, sliced thinly
675 g (1½ lb) lemons, sliced thinly
1.7 litres (3 pints) water
175 g (6 oz) raisins
2.7 kg (6 lb) granulated sugar
rum (see step 3)

1 Place the citrus fruits in a preserving pan, with the water and the raisins, and bring to the boil.
2 Simmer slowly for 2 hours, until the peel is very tender.
3 Add the sugar and boil to setting point (see page 21). Remove any scum (see page 21).
4 Put 2 teaspoons of rum per 450 g (1 lb) into the cooled, sterilised jars (page 16). Pour the marmalade into the jars containing the measured rum. Seal (page 22), label and store.

CLAIRE MACDONALD'S CITRUS FRUIT MARMALADE

675 g (1½ lb) seville oranges
675 g (1½ lb) other citrus fruit, e.g., a grapefruit, a sweet orange and the balance of the weight made up with tangerines or clementines, but not satsumas
2.2 litres (4 pints) water
2.7 kg (6 lb) granulated or preserving sugar

1 Place the fruit in a large saucepan or jam pan with the water and simmer gently for 2–3 hours, or until the peel is very soft.
2 Remove the fruit from the pan, leaving the cooking liquid, and, when cool enough to handle, cut each orange, grapefruit or tangerine in half. Scoop out all the pips into a small saucepan.
3 Cover with another 300 ml (½ pint) of water and simmer for 10 minutes. Leave to cool, and then strain this liquid into the jam pan, with the liquid that the fruit was cooked in. (Make sure that you press out all of the liquid from the solids in the sieve.)
4 While the pips are simmering, cut up the fruit or use a food processor. Put the cut-up fruit back in the jam pan. Add the sugar and cook on a low heat, stirring occasionally, until the sugar has completely dissolved. Remove any scum (see page 21).
5 Now boil furiously; after 10 minutes, pull the pan off the heat to test the marmalade for a set (see page 21). If not ready, boil again for 5 minutes and test again.
6 When a set is achieved, pour into cooled, sterilised jars and seal (see pages 16 and 22). Label and store.

MAKES: about 2.2 kg (5 lb)
PREPARATION TIME: about 45 minutes + 1 week standing

This recipe is from Claire Macdonald's book *Sweet Things* and combines all the usual mincemeat ingredients but without the addition of treacle and other items that can mask the fruity flavours. Claire comments what a world of difference there is between a home-made mincemeat and a commercial sort.

There are endless variations to mincemeat, so feel free to put your own mark on the recipe. I love apricots in anything and some folk like to add red and green glacé cherries for a more festive look. I usually substitute these for the mixed peel in any recipe as my family doesn't like peel. I have also seen several versions with cranberries, which you could add in place of some of the apple. There are several puddings in which mincemeat features and a home-made variety makes them all the more sumptuous.

MAKES: about 1.8 kg (4 lb)
PREPARATION TIME: 20 minutes
COOKING TIME: 20 minutes

I discovered this recipe in a magazine years ago and have made it every year since. It is very quick and easy to make and I store it in a large polythene tub. It contains no added sugar or fat but, of course, the dried fruit has a high sugar content and may also have a coating of oil. It's a far cry from the mincemeat I remember my mother making, which contained real meat (usually beef or tongue), which is why recipes nowadays often contain beef suet in place of the meat.

CLAIRE MACDONALD'S MINCEMEAT

350 g (12 oz) raisins
225 g (8 oz) sultanas
225 g (8 oz) currants
115 g (4 oz) chopped mixed peel
115 g (4 oz) chopped blanched almonds
225 g (8 oz) shredded suet
   (beef or vegetarian)
450 g (1 lb) dark muscovado sugar
350 g (12 oz) apples, cored and chopped
   (Claire uses Cox's apples)
grated zest of 2 lemons
juice of 1 lemon
grated zest of 2 oranges
juice of 1 orange
115 ml (4 fl oz) brandy
1 teaspoon ground cinnamon
1 rounded teaspoon grated nutmeg
1 rounded teaspoon ground allspice

1   Mix all the ingredients together in a large, non-metallic bowl. Cover with cling film and leave for a week, giving the occasional stir.
2   After a week, pot into cooled, sterilised jars and cover (see pages 16 and 22). Keep for a further 2 weeks before using.

CHRISTMAS MINCEMEAT

900 g (2 lb) mixed dried fruit
450 g (1 lb) cooking apples, peeled
   and grated
2 teaspoons ground mixed spice
575 ml (1 pint) medium-sweet or dry cider
50 g (2 oz) hazelnuts, chopped (optional)
2 tablespoons brandy

1   Simmer the dried fruits, apples and spice in the cider for about 20 minutes, or until the fruit is pulpy and most of the liquid has evaporated.
2   Stir in the hazelnuts and brandy.
3   Pack into cooled, sterilised jars and cover with a waxed disc and cellophane cover (see pages 16 and 22) or store in a polythene tub. Keep in a cool place or the refrigerator until required. It keeps for up to 4 months.

RUBY RED GRAPEFRUIT MARMALADE *pictured opposite*

MAKES: 2.2–2.7 kg (5–6 lb)
PREPARATION TIME: 30 minutes
COOKING TIME: about 3 hours

900 g (2 lb) ruby red grapefruit, washed
and quartered
1 lemon, washed and quartered
1.1 litres (2 pints) water
1.8 kg (4 lb) granulated sugar

This seems to be a very popular variety, going by the number of recipes around. The added colour of the fruit gives a lovely blush to the finished marmalade, so try to find the ruby red variety rather than just a pink one. You could also use the ingredients for Claire Macdonald's Citrus Fruit Marmalade (page 64), cooking the fruit whole and boiling the pips and peel separately.

1 Remove the pulp from the peel of the grapefruit and lemon. Remove the pips and tie them in a muslin bag. If the peel is really thick, remove most of the pith and put it in the bag also.
2 Cut all the peel finely and place in a large preserving pan, with the chopped pulp, bag of pips and water. Bring to the boil and then simmer until the peel is soft, 1–2 hours.
3 Remove the muslin bag. Add the sugar and stir until dissolved. Bring to the boil and boil rapidly until setting point is reached – about 20–30 minutes (see page 22). Remove any scum (see page 22).
4 Pour into cooled, sterilised jars and seal (see pages 16 and 22). Label and store.

GINGER & GRAPEFRUIT MARMALADE: Add 2 teaspoons of ground ginger and 115 g (4 oz) of chopped crystallised ginger or stem ginger preserved in syrup at the initial cooking stage.

TIPSY GRAPEFRUIT MARMALADE: Add 4 tablespoons of any spirit or liqueur (try whisky, brandy, rum or how about Campari or a liqueur?) just before potting.

HOME-MADE GENTLEMAN'S RELISH

MAKES: 225 g (8 oz)
PREPARATION TIME: 15 minutes

3 x 50 g cans of anchovy fillets
6 tablespoons milk
150 g (5 oz) unsalted butter
freshly ground black and cayenne pepper

This is Sue Jones' Dad's favourite and she always make him some each Christmas for his tree present.

1 Drain the anchovy fillets and soak in the milk for 10 minutes.
2 Drain off the milk and put the anchovies in a food processor, with the butter and seasoning.
3 Purée to a smooth paste. Pot into small cooled, sterilised jars, seal and store in the fridge for up to 3 weeks.

MAKES: about 1.3 kg (3 lb)
PREPARATION TIME: 15 minutes
COOKING TIME: about 1¼ hours + 10 minutes standing

CITRUS FRUIT MICROWAVE MARMALADE

This is another recipe tried and tested on the 'Preserves' course at Denman College – you can use any combination of citrus fruit but stick to the given amounts. You could add additional flavourings such as those suggested in the variations to Traditional Seville Orange Marmalade (page 63).

I use an 800-Watt microwave; check your manufacturer's instructions for advice on adapting timings for ovens with different ratings.

675 g (1½ lb) citrus fruit, washed, quartered
and pips removed and reserved
450 ml (15 fl oz) water
1.3 kg (3 lb) sugar

1 Place the prepared fruit in a food processor and whizz until chopped to the consistency you prefer – chunky or smooth.

2 Place in a large bowl suitable for the microwave, with the water. Put the pips in a muslin bag and add to the bowl. Cook on full power for 15 minutes.

3 Stir in the sugar and microwave on medium power for 60 minutes or until setting point is reached, stirring thoroughly every 10 minutes. Remove any scum (see page 21).

4 Allow to stand for 10 minutes and then remove the bag of pips. Pour into cooled, sterilised jars and seal (see pages 16 and 22). Label and store.

MAKES: about 1.3 kg (3 lb)
PREPARATION TIME: 30 minutes
COOKING TIME: about 15 minutes + standing overnight

WOW (WALNUT, ORANGE & WHISKY) MINCEMEAT

I found this recipe whilst searching for ideas to use for a WI Federation Christmas event. Needless to say, this was a very popular variety and has since become a firm favourite. You could substitute cranberries for half the apple, for a sharper taste.

450 g (1 lb) cooking apples, peeled and chopped
225 g (8 oz) sultanas
225 g (8 oz) currants
115 g (4 oz) candied peel
115 g (4 oz) walnut pieces
175 g (6 oz) melted butter or suet
225 g (8 oz) light muscovado sugar
juice and grated zest of 1 large orange
1 teaspoon ground cinnamon
½ teaspoon grated nutmeg
½ teaspoon ground cloves
4 tablespoons whisky

1 Cook the apples with 4 tablespoons of water until pulpy. Mash down and allow to cool.

2 Add the rest of the ingredients and mix well. Allow to stand overnight.

3 Pack into cooled, sterilised jars and cover with waxed discs and cellophane covers (see pages 16 and 22), or store in a polythene tub with a lid.

MAKES: about 4.5 kg (10 lb)
PREPARATION TIME: about 1 hour
COOKING TIME: 20 minutes

CARIBBEAN MARMALADE

Glenys Gibson's idea for this came after a trip to the Caribbean, seeing all the citrus fruit growing there and being given a bottle of black rum to bring home. Glenys thought it would bring back memories of a wonderful trip, which it certainly did, and this is now one of her most popular marmalades. Sadly, she has to get the rum from the supermarket and not Barbados!

1.5 kg (3 lb 5 oz) mixture of grapefruit, oranges, lemons and 2 limes
2 litres (3½ pints) water
3 kg (6½ lb) granulated sugar
black rum – it needs to be black and rough for the flavour (see step 3)

1   Slice up all the fruit and remove the pips. Place in a large pan with the water and simmer until the peel is very soft. Take particular care that the lime peel is very tender, as it can become chewy when sugar is added otherwise. This can also be cooked in a large casserole in the oven. It is also very successful done in a slow-cooker overnight but reduce the amount of water used, remembering to add the remainder when you transfer to a preserving pan.
2   Transfer the fruit and liquid to a preserving pan. if necessary, and add the sugar, stirring until dissolved. Bring to a full rolling boil and test for a set (see page 21) after 5 minutes. It does set quite quickly – usually within 10 minutes. Remove any scum (see page 21).
3   In the bottom of each of the cooled, sterilised jars (see page 16), put 2 teaspoons of rum per 450 g (1 lb). When the marmalade is poured in to fill the jar, the rum mixes in and gives a better flavour than if it was added to the jam pan.
4   Seal (see page 22) and label.

MAKES: 1.3 kg (3 lb)
PREPARATION TIME: 20 minutes
COOKING TIME: 1–1½ hours

CRANBERRY CHUTNEY *pictured on page 11*

This makes a lovely and colourful accompaniment to traditional Christmas fare and would make a very acceptable gift.

25 g (1 oz) butter
350 g (12 oz) onions, chopped
450 g (1 lb) cooking apples, peeled and sliced
1 teaspoon ground mixed spice
350 g (12 oz) fresh or frozen cranberries
450 g (1 lb) light soft brown sugar
425 ml (15 fl oz) white malt vinegar

1   Melt the butter in a large saucepan. Add the onions, apples and spice and cook until the onions are soft – about 20 minutes.
2   Add the cranberries and sugar and stir until the sugar is dissolved. Add the vinegar and bring to the boil, stirring occasionally.
3   Reduce the heat and simmer for 1–1½ hours, until the chutney is reduced to a thick consistency.
4   Spoon into cooled, sterilised jars and cover with a vinegar-proof lid (see pages 16 and 22). Label and store for 4–6 weeks before using.

MAKES: 350 g (12 oz)
PREPARATION TIME: 20 minutes
COOKING TIME: about 20 minutes

This is another recipe from Claire Macdonald, from her book *More Seasonal Cooking*. Claire makes this curd to fold into whipped cream as a filling for meringues or sponge cakes, as well as a spread for the breakfast toast or scones for tea. Don't try it with ordinary sweet oranges – you need the tang and full orange flavour of the seville.

I make this in the microwave, to cut down on the cooking time: see Lemon Curd (page 24) for method.

MAKES: about 2.7 kg (6 lb)
PREPARATION TIME: 20 minutes
COOKING TIME: 10 minutes in pressure cooker and 15–20 minutes in open pan

Cooking marmalade in a pressure cooker considerably shortens the process of softening the peel. The same method can be used for other citrus-fruit marmalades, such as grapefruit, three-fruit or lime and lemon. It may be as well to check with the instructions for your pressure cooker for any specific information.

SEVILLE ORANGE CURD

SEVILLE ORANGE MARMALADE MADE IN A PRESSURE COOKER

2 large whole eggs, plus 2 large egg yolks
115 g (4 oz) butter, preferably unsalted, cubed
115 g (4 oz) caster sugar
grated zest and juice of 2 seville oranges

1 In a jug, beat together the whole eggs and egg yolks, and then sieve them into a bowl.
2 Add the butter, sugar and orange zest and juice. Put the bowl over a saucepan of gently simmering water, and stir occasionally (there's no need to stir continuously) until the curd is really thick.
3 Take the bowl off the heat and spoon the curd into cooled, sterilised jars (see pages 16 and 22) or store in a covered bowl. Leave to cool. Store in the refrigerator.

900 g (2 lb) oranges, washed and scrubbed, halved, juice squeezed and reserved
2 lemons, prepared as for oranges
1.1 litres (2 pints) water
1.8 kg (4 lb) sugar

1 Cut the fruit into quarters and scrape out the remaining pulp and membrane. Put this, together with the fruit pips, in a muslin bag and tie loosely.
2 Place the fruit, the juices, the bag of pips and 575 ml (1 pint) of the water in the pressure cooker. Bring to medium (10 lb) pressure and cook for 10 minutes.
3 Reduce the pressure quickly and cool sufficiently to handle the fruit.
4 Discard the lemon and shred, slice or process the orange peel.
5 Squeeze the muslin bag really well to extract all the juice. Put the juice back into the cooker with another 575 ml (1 pint) of water and the prepared peel.
6 Bring to the boil in the open pan on a high heat. Add the sugar and stir until completely dissolved. Boil rapidly until setting point is reached (see page 21).
7 Pour into cooled, sterilised jars and seal (see pages 16 and 22). Label and store.

From left to right: Banana Chutney (page 73); Pink Grapefruit & Cranberry Marmalade (page 75)

ALL YEAR ROUND PRESERVES

MAKES: about 450 g (1 lb)
PREPARATION TIME: 15 minutes
COOKING TIME: about 40 minutes

This is another of Christine Sherriff's recipes that do not contain added sugar. Christine suggests that a good way of cleaning the skins of oranges and lemons is to scrub well in a solution of 1 tablespoon of cider vinegar to 575 ml (1 pint) of water. Rinse well and use as required.

ORANGE & LEMON MARMALADE

peel of 1 orange, sliced finely
peel of 1 lemon, sliced finely
425 ml (15 fl oz) freshly squeezed orange
   juice (commercial heat-treated
   orange juice is not suitable)
300 ml (^{1}/$_2$ pint) apple juice concentrate
   (from healthfood shops)

1 Place the orange and lemon peels in a saucepan with the orange juice and simmer gently until the rind is soft – about 30 minutes.
2 Add the apple juice and continue to boil for 10 minutes. Test for a set. Remove any scum (see page 21).
3 When setting point is reached (see page 21), pour into cooled, sterilised jars and cover (see pages 16 and 22). Label and store in the refrigerator.

MAKES: about 2.2 kg (5 lb)
PREPARATION TIME:
15 minutes + overnight soaking
COOKING TIME: 30 minutes

Another of Judi Binn's recipes is a useful standby for the winter when the fruit is finished and the store is empty. Judi reckons it makes a great filling for pancakes and also a topping for ice cream – sounds good to me, too!

TANGIER JAM

225 g (8 oz) dried apricots, chopped
450 g (1 lb) raisins
450 g (1 lb) dates, chopped
450 g (1 lb) peeled weight bananas, chopped
1.8 kg (4 lb) light soft brown sugar

1 Cover the apricots and raisins with water and leave to soak overnight.
2 Drain away the water and place all the fruit in a large preserving pan. Simmer for 15 minutes.
3 Add the sugar and stir until dissolved.
4 Bring to the boil and boil rapidly for about 10 minutes or until setting point is reached (see page 21). Remove any scum (see page 21).
5 Pot into cooled, sterilised jars, seal and label (see pages 16 and 22).

MAKES: about 675 g (1^1/$_2$ lb)
PREPARATION TIME: 20 minutes
COOKING TIME: 30 minutes

This recipe needs no added sugar but, instead, uses apple juice in concentrated form, which you can buy from healthfood shops. Christine Sherriff makes it regularly for someone who is diabetic but, obviously, individual diabetics' dietary needs vary greatly. It is not a true preserve as it is too low in sugar to prevent moulds from growing. Store in a refrigerator.

MIXED BERRY JAM

225 g (8 oz) strawberries,
   fresh or frozen, hulled
225 g (8 oz) blackberries, fresh or frozen
225 g (8 oz) gooseberries
225 g (8 oz) apple juice concentrate,
   weighed in a plastic container

1 Liquidise half the fruit and place in a saucepan, with the whole fruit.
2 Simmer gently until the gooseberries are cooked – about 15–20 minutes.
3 Add the apple juice and boil for 15 minutes or until you achieve a set (see page 21). Remove any scum (see page 21).
4 Pour into cooled, sterilised jars and cover (see pages 16 and 22). Label and store for up to 6 months. Once open, store in the fridge and use within 2 weeks.

MAKES: about 3.6 kg (9 lb)
PREPARATION TIME: 30 minutes
COOKING TIME: 1–1½ hours

This chutney was the result of a **'happy accident'** – so says Sue Prickett of Hutton Roof in Lancashire and a producer for Kirkby Lonsdale WI Market. Someone gave Sue some very cheap bananas which were 'past their best'. Sue says that 'very ripe' bananas give a far better flavour than under-ripe ones anyway. Sue buys peppers when they are cheaper, chops them and freezes them in the quantities she needs for her recipes, which helps save time and cuts the cost too. This is very similar to one of the recipes given to me by Liz Dawson-Margrave but that one does without the peppers and raisins and includes a fresh green chilli, sliced finely.

MAKES: 225–350 g (8–12 oz)
PREPARATION & COOKING TIME:
about 30 minutes

Another useful recipe for using up orange peel that would otherwise be discarded. Use as a garnish or decoration for dishes containing oranges.

SPILLIKINS

BANANA CHUTNEY *pictured on page 71*

115 g (4 oz) sugar
thinly pared zest of 2 oranges

1 Dissolve the sugar in 300 ml (½ pint) of water and then bring to the boil and boil for 3 minutes.
2 Cut the peeled zest into strips – matchstick thickness. Place in a pan with cold water to cover and bring to the boil. Strain.
3 Reboil in fresh water, strain and add to the sugar syrup. Bring to the boil and simmer for 5 minutes.
4 Pour into a cooled, sterilised jar and cover with a twist-top (see pages 16 and 22). Label and store in a cool, dry place, for up to 6 months. Once open, use within 2–3 weeks.

1.8 kg (4 lb) bananas, chopped
4 peppers, chopped
4 onions, chopped
450 g (1 lb) raisins
1.1 litres (2 pints) malt vinegar
4 garlic cloves, crushed
2 teaspoons salt
½ teaspoon pepper
4 teaspoons curry powder
2 teaspoons ground turmeric
a pinch of ground cloves
900 g (2 lb) sugar
cornflour, if necessary (see step 2)

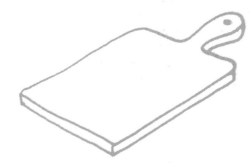

1 Cook everything, except the sugar and cornflour, together until soft and pulpy – about 1 hour.
2 Add the sugar and cook until the vinegar is reduced. Thicken with a little cornflour, slaked in a small amount of cold water, if necessary.
3 Spoon into cooled, sterilised jars, seal and label (see pages 16 and 22). Store for 6–8 weeks before using.

MAKES: enough to fill five or six 75 cl bottles
PREPARATION TIME: about 15 minutes + 24 hours + 5 days + 3 weeks + 6 months + 3 months

NEAR-MISS JAM WINE

I had never heard of wine made from jam before but it's a great idea – thanks to Ann Creasey. Ann says it certainly saves face, as well as the jam. All the ingredients are available from home-brewing shops and some pharmacies.

1.3 kg (3 lb) any fruit jam with soft set or no set
1 teaspoon pectin-destroying enzyme (see note)
2 teaspoons citric acid
225 g (8 oz) raisins, minced or processed
675 g (1½ lb) sugar
1 teaspoon grape tannin
1 teaspoon brewer's yeast
1 yeast nutrient tablet
1 Camden tablet, crushed

1   Put the jam into a sterilised plastic bucket and pour over the 4.5 litres (1 gallon) of boiling water. Leave to cool.
2   Add pectin-destroying enzyme and citric acid. Leave for 24 hours.
3   Add the minced raisins, sugar, tannin, yeast and yeast nutrient tablet. Stir well to dissolve the sugar. Cover and leave to ferment for about 5 days, giving it a stir each day.
4   Strain the mixture through a nylon sieve or muslin into a fermentation jar. Fit an airlock and leave to ferment out, i.e. until the bubbling stops – about 3 weeks.
5   When fermentation is finished and the wine is clear, rack into a clean jar for 6 months storage, adding the crushed Camden tablet to prevent further fermentation.
6   Bottle after another 3 months.

NOTE: Using pectin-destroying enzyme – Pectinol or Pektolase – is most important, since the high level of pectin that jam contains would otherwise prevent the wine from clearing.

MAKES: about 2.2 kg (5 lb)
PREPARATION TIME: 30 minutes
COOKING TIME: about 1 hour

STORECUPBOARD CHUTNEY

The ingredients for this recipe can vary, depending on the type of dried fruit you have in your cupboard at the time of making. This is another of Terry Clarke's recipes – Terry is a stalwart cook for Southwell WI Market. We swapped many a recipe on our train journeys down to London for WI Market meetings!

675 g (1½ lb) mixed dried fruit, e.g., apricots, dates, figs, peaches, prunes, sultanas, etc.
1.3 kg (3 lb) cooking apples, peeled and chopped
450 g (1 lb) onions, chopped
675 g (1½ lb) soft brown sugar
6 garlic cloves, crushed or chopped
50 g (2 oz) fresh root ginger, finely chopped
2–4 dried chillies, crushed
850 ml (1½ pints) cider vinegar

1   Cut the dried fruit into even-sized pieces.
2   Mix everything together in a large preserving pan and bring to the boil, stirring well.
3   Simmer the mixture over a medium heat until very thick, stirring regularly – about 45 minutes.
4   Spoon into cooled, sterilised jars and seal with vinegar-proof tops (see pages 16 and 22). Label and store for 6–8 weeks before using.

MAKES: about 4.5 kg (10 lb)
PREPARATION TIME: 30 minutes
COOKING TIME: 2 hours

PINK GRAPEFRUIT & CRANBERRY MARMALADE *pictured on page 71*

This recipe was devised by Glenys Gibson, following a visit to a friend in Florida who has a huge pink grapefruit tree in her front garden. Put that together with the Americans' love for cranberries and you have a wonderful and colourful marmalade. Glenys first brought dried cranberries back from America but they are now readily available in most supermarkets and other outlets, on the dried vine-fruit shelf.

1.5 kg (3 lb 5 oz) pink grapefruit, sliced, pips removed
150 g (5 oz) dried cranberries
2 litres (3½ pints) water
juice of 1 lemon or 2 teaspoons citric acid
3 kg (6½ lb) sugar

1 Place the sliced grapefruit and the cranberries, with the water and the lemon juice or citric acid, in a large saucepan and simmer, covered, until the peel is very tender. This can also be done in a large casserole in the oven. It is also very successful done in a slow-cooker overnight but reduce the amount of water used, remembering to add the remainder when you transfer to a preserving pan.
2 Transfer the fruit and liquid to a large preserving pan and add the sugar, stirring until dissolved. Bring to a full rolling boil and test for a set after 5 minutes. It does set quite quickly – usually within 10 minutes (see page 21). Remove any scum (see page 21).
3 Pour into cooled, sterilised jars, seal and label (see pages 16 and 22).

MAKES: about 1.3 kg (3 lb)
PREPARATION TIME:
overnight soaking + about 20 minutes
COOKING TIME: 30 minutes

MEDICINAL JAM

This title may sound off-putting but it really is a delicious jam and you do feel that it is doing you some good as you eat it. It is sometimes known as 'All the Year Round Jam' as it is made from dried fruits and nuts which, of course, are always available.

115 g (4 oz) whole almonds,
    blanched and chopped
450 g (1 lb) prunes
    (preferably ready-pitted prunes)
450 g (1 lb) raisins
450 g (1 lb) demerara sugar

1 Put the nuts and fruit in a bowl and pour on 575 ml (1 pint) of water. Leave to soak overnight.
2 Next day, strain off the water and keep to one side. Chop the prunes and raisins and then place everything, including the reserved water, in a large preserving pan.
3 Heat gently, stirring continuously until all the sugar is dissolved.
4 Bring to the boil and cook rapidly until setting point is reached – about 20 minutes (see page 21). Remove any scum (see page 21).
5 Pour into cooled, sterilised jars, seal and label (see pages 16 and 22).

MAKES: about 4.5 kg (10 lb)
PREPARATION TIME: 20 minutes
COOKING TIME: 40 minutes

ALLEN'S CITRUS-FRUIT MARMALADE

I have come across several recipes for using surplus peel from citrus fruits that has been stored in the freezer until you have sufficient weight – such as '**Pennywise Marmalade**' and '**Miser's Marmalade**'.

However, the nicest one must be the one in the 1995 WI Markets cookbook, which was developed by Allen Wood of Nottingham WI Market. Allen is loathe to throw away surplus grapefruit and orange peel. It can be made at any time of the year and is truly delicious. Allen adds whole lemons and just the flesh of limes, which I think is the secret of the lovely flavour. Allen also favours using the pressure cooker to soften the peel, which, of course, is also a very economical method of cooking.

675 g (1½ lb) mixed orange, grapefruit and lemon peel, washed
450 g (1 lb) whole lemons
225 g (8 oz) lime flesh only (no peel)
300 ml (½ pint) water
2.7 kg (6 lb) sugar

1 Place the peel with the water in the pressure cooker and cook for 10 minutes at 15 lb pressure. Leave to cool to room temperature.
2 Drain, retaining the liquid, and slice the peel thinly when cool enough to handle. Set aside.
3 Cut the lemons into quarters, remove the pips and place these in a muslin bag. Remove and roughly chop the flesh; slice the peel thinly. Place in the pressure cooker.
4 Add the lime pips and peel to the lemon pips in the muslin bag. Chop the lime flesh roughly and add to the pressure cooker.
5 Add another 300 ml (½ pint) of water and cook for 10 minutes at 15 lb pressure. Allow to cool to room temperature.
6 Place the previously cooked peel and the lemon and lime peel together in a large preserving pan. Squeeze the muslin bag thoroughly, to extract all the juice. Mix together all the retained juices and add sufficient water to make up to 1.4 litres (2½ pints). Add to the preserving pan, along with the sugar.
7 Heat until the sugar is dissolved. Bring to the boil and boil until setting point is reached (see page 21). Remove any scum (see page 21).
8 Pour into cooled, sterilised jars, seal and label (see pages 16 and 22).

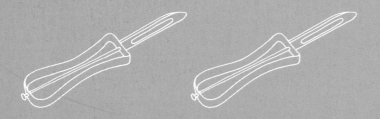

Edith Calvert, of Chapel-St-Leonards WI Market and a former Society Chairman, sent me these variations, using commercially prepared oranges or lemons.

MARMALADE MADE FROM COMMERCIALLY PREPARED FRUIT

LEMON (OR ORANGE) & PINEAPPLE MARMALADE

MAKES: six or seven 450 g (1 lb) jars
PREPARATION & COOKING TIME: about 1 hour

1 can of commercially prepared lemons (or oranges)
1 tablespoon lemon juice
230 g can of pineapple in own juice
1.8 kg (4 lb) sugar

1   Strain and chop the pineapple (Edith uses a food processor).
2   Make the fruit juice up to 410 ml (14 fl oz) with water.
3   Add to the marmalade and sugar in a large bowl and make up according to the instructions on the can.
4   Pot and seal (see pages 16 and 22).

ORANGE (OR LEMON) & GRAPEFRUIT MARMALADE

MAKES: six or seven 450 g (1 lb) jars
PREPARATION & COOKING TIME: about 1 hour

1 can of commercially prepared oranges
540 g can of grapefruit segments in own juice
2 kg (4½ lb) sugar

1   Strain and chop the grapefruit. Make the juice up to 550 ml (scant 1 pint) with water.
2   Add to the marmalade and sugar and make up following the instructions on the can.
3   Pot and seal (see pages 16 and 22).

TIPSY MARMALADE: To each jar, add 1–2 tablespoons of whisky, brandy or your favourite liqueur and then fill with the hot marmalade mixture made according to the instructions on the can.

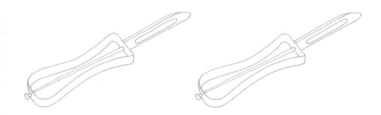

Allen's citrus fruit marmalade **76**

apple curd, bramble and **44**

apple jelly:
> rowan berry and **42**; rowan berry and rosemary and **42**; spiced **43**

apricots, dried:
> apricot and marrow chutney **54**; apricot and orange marmalade **62**; Tangier jam **72**

apricots, fresh:
> apricot and honey conserve **32**; brandied grape and apricot jam **31**

Aunt Mary's green tomato chutney **50**

autumn marmalade **44**

banana chutney **73**

beetroot and ginger chutney **46**

beetroot jam, orange and **47**

blackberries:
> bramble and apple curd **44**; blackberry and sloe jelly **60**

blackcurrant jam, rhubarb and **28**

bramble and apple curd **44**

brandied grape and apricot jam **31**

Caribbean marmalade **69**

celery chutney, red tomato and **50**

Christmas mincemeat **65**

chutney:
> apricot and marrow **54**; and walnut **54**; banana **73**; beetroot and ginger **46**; cranberry **69**; Diana's uncooked **46**; Easter **25**; gooseberry **35**; green tomato, Aunt Mary's **50**; Jane's mango **42**; nectarine **30**; orchard cottage **55**; pumpkin **57**; ratatouille **30**; red tomato and celery **50**; rhubarb and date **28**; rhubarb and apricot, raisin or sultana **28**; rhubarb and garlic **28**; rhubarb and ginger **28**; South Seas **38**; spiced plum **57**; storecupboard **74**

cinnamon grape pickle **51**

citrus fruit marmalade, Allen's **78**

citrus fruit marmalade, Claire Macdonald's **64**

citrus fruit microwave marmalade **68**

Claire Macdonald's citrus fruit marmalade **64**

Claire Macdonald's mincemeat **65**

conserve, apricot and honey **32**

conserve, strawberry **36**

cordial, elderflower **35**

cranberry chutney **69**

cranberry curd **62**

Cumberland bean pickle **56**

curd:
> bramble and apple **44**; cranberry **62**; elderflower **24**; gooseberry **35**; lemon **24**; passion fruit **24**; seville orange **70**; West Country **53**

Diana's uncooked chutney **46**

dried apricots see apricots, dried

Dylan's pickled walnuts **40**

Easter chutney **25**

elderflower cordial **35**

elderflower curd **24**

elderflower jam, strawberry and **36**

exotic fruits jam **62**

figs, dried:
> rhubarb and fig jam **26**

gentleman's relish, home-made **66**

geranium plum jam **42**

gooseberry chutney **35**

gooseberry curd **35**

gooseberry jam, strawberry and **36**

gooseberry mint jelly **39**

grape and apricot jam, brandied **31**

grapefruit marmalade:
> lemon and **77**; orange and **77**; ruby red **66**

grapefruit, pink, and cranberry, marmalade **75**

grapes:
> cinnamon grape pickle **51**; plum, grape and cardamom jelly **48**

green tomato chutney, Aunt Mary's **50**

hedgerow jam **52**

high dumpsy dearie jam **47**

home-made gentleman's relish **66**

honey conserve, apricot and **32**

honey, spiced, orange slices in **60**

ice cream, lemon curd **24**

jam:
> rhubarb, orange and candied peel **26**; brandied grape and apricot **31**; exotic fruits **62**; four-fruit **38**; geranium; plum **42**; hedgerow **52**; high dumpsy dearie **47**; medicinal **75**; microwave strawberry, with apple **34**; midsummer **38**; mixed berry **72**; orange and beetroot **47**; orchard **52**; plum and mulled wine **56**; rhubarb and blackcurrant **28**; rhubarb and fig **26**; rhubarb and orange **26**; Tangier **72**; traditional raspberry **32**; traditional strawberry **36**; tutti frutti **38**

Jane's mango chutney **42**

jelly:
> blackberry and sloe **60**; gooseberry mint **39**; plum, grape and cardamom **48**; rowan berry and apple **42**; rowan berry and rosemary apple **42**; spiced apple **43**

lemon curd **24**

lemon curd ice cream **24**

lemon marmalade, orange and **72**

lemongrass jam, strawberry and **36**

liqueur, strawberry jam with **36**

mango chutney, Jane's **42**

mango pickle **53**

marmalade made from commercially prepared fruit:
> lemon and pineapple; orange and pineapple; orange and grapefruit; lemon and grapefruit **77**

marmalade:
> Allen's citrus fruit **78**; apricot and orange **62**; autumn **44**; Caribbean **69**; citrus fruit

microwave **68**; coriander **63**; black treacle **63**; boozy **63**; nutty **63**; extra-fruity **63**; ginger **63**; orange and lemon **72**; peach **31**; pink grapefruit and cranberry **75**; pumpkin **43**; ruby red grapefruit **66**; rum and raisin **64**; seville orange, made in a pressure cooker **70**; tipsy **77**; traditional seville orange **63**

marrow chutney, apricot and **54**

medicinal jam **75**

microwave marmalade, citrus fruit **68**

microwave strawberry jam with apple **34**

mincemeat, Christmas **65**

mincemeat, Claire Macdonald's **65**

mincemeat, WOW (walnut orange and whisky) **68**

mint jelly, gooseberry **39**

mixed berry jam **72**

mustard pickles:
mostarda di frutta **58**; piccalilli **58**

near-miss jam wine **74**

nectarine chutney **30**

orange and beetroot jam **47**

orange and lemon marmalade **72**

orange marmalade, apricot and **62**

orange marmalade, traditional seville **63**

orange slices in spiced honey **60**

orange zest, candied: spillikins **73**

oranges, seville see seville oranges

orchard cottage chutney **55**

orchard jam **52**

passion fruit curd **24**

passion fruit jam, strawberry and **36**

peach marmalade **31**

pears, spiced, in raspberry vinegar **51**

piccalilli **58**

pickle:
cinnamon grape **51**; Cumberland bean **56**; mango **53**; piccalilli **58**

pickled walnuts, Dylan's **40**

pineapple marmalade:
lemon and **77**; orange and **77**

pink grapefruit and cranberry marmalade **75**

plums:
geranium plum jam **42**; plum and mulled wine jam **56**; plum pot **48**; plum, grape and cardamom jelly **48**; spiced plum chutney **57**

pressure cooker, seville orange marmalade made in a **70**

pumpkin chutney **57**

pumpkin marmalade **43**

raspberry jam, traditional **32**

raspberry vinegar **34**

ratatouille chutney **30**

red tomato and celery chutney **50**

redcurrant jam, strawberry and **36**

relish, home-made gentleman's **66**

rhubarb and blackcurrant jam **28**

rhubarb and fig jam **26**

rhubarb and orange jam **26**

rhubarb chutney:
and date **28**; and garlic **28**; and ginger **28**; and apricot, sultana or raisin **28**

rhubarb jam, strawberry and **36**

rhubarb, orange and candied peel jam **26**

rowan berry and apple jelly **42**

ruby red grapefruit marmalade **66**

rum and raisin marmalade **64**

runner beans:
Cumberland bean pickle **56**

seville oranges:
Claire Macdonald's citrus fruit marmalade **64**; seville orange curd **70**; seville orange marmalade made in a pressure cooker **70**; traditional seville orange marmalade **63**

sloe jelly, blackberry and **60**

South Seas chutney **38**

spiced apple jelly **43**

spiced pears in raspberry vinegar **51**

spiced plum chutney **57**

spillikins **73**

storecupboard chutney **74**

strawberry conserve **36**

strawberry jam:
microwave, with apple **34**; traditional **36**; and elderflower **36**; lemon grass **36**; liqueur **36**; gooseberry **36**; rhubarb **36**; redcurrant **36**; passion fruit **36**

Tangier jam **72**

tipsy marmalade **77**

traditional raspberry jam 32:
and nectarine (or peach) **32**; and rhubarb **32**

traditional seville orange marmalade **63**

traditional strawberry jam **36**

tutti frutti jam **34**

uncooked chutney, Diana's **46**

vinegar, raspberry **34**

walnuts, Dylan's pickled **40**

West Country curd **53**

wine, near-miss jam **74**

WOW (walnut, orange and whisky) mincemeat **68**

Julian Graves Ltd
Unit 95
Second Avenue
Pensnett Trading Estate
Kingswinford
West Midlands
DY6 7FT
Telephone : **0138 428 2700**
Excellent range of quality fruits and nuts at reasonable prices. 80 shops around the UK and 22 franchise outlets. Telephone for a list of outlets and range of products.

Lakeland Limited
Alexandra Buildings
Windermere
Cumbria
LA23 1BQ
Telephone: **0153 948 8100**
Fax: **0153 948 8300**
www.lakelandlimited.com
Family-run business selling a huge range of home, kitchen and general storage equipment. Very good range of preserve-making equipment and accessories. Comprehensive mail-order catalogue, over 20 stores around the country and a very easy to use telephone and/or online ordering system.

National Federation of Women's Institutes
104 New Kings Road
London
SW6 4LY
Telephone: **020 7371 9300**

USEFUL ADDRESSES

Harrison Smith French Flint Ltd
Rich House
40 Crimscott Street
London
SE1 5TE
Telephone : **020 7231 6777**
Good range of glass jars in small quantities— you don't have to buy 1000! Very helpful and friendly advice when you phone.

BigBarn
Telephone: **01234 871 005**
www.bigbarn.co.uk
A virtual marketplace, allowing consumers to find high-quality, local, safe food. You simply type in your postcode to see a map of your area, showing icons representing producers and the type of goods they sell. There are over 3000 icons on the map, including the local WI Markets.

Diabetes UK
(formerly, the British Diabetic Association)
10 Queen Anne Street
London
W1M 0BD
Telephone: **020 7323 1531**
www.diabetes.org.uk
The website contains useful information on adapting recipes and information on recipe books.

HMSO Publications
The Stationery Office Ltd
PO Box 29
Norwich
NR3 1GN
Telephone: **0870 600 5522**

WI Country Markets Ltd
183a Oxford Road
Reading
Berkshire
RG1 7XA
Telephone: **0118 939 4646**
Email: info@wimarkets.co.uk
www.wimarkets.co.uk
Excellent outlets for selling your home-made preserves and other home produce to your local community. Send for a free list of WI Markets throughout England, Wales and the Islands. Shop at your local WI Market and send a parcel of goods for any occasion.